FROM MANET TO GAUGUIN

Masterpieces from Swiss Private Collections

Royal Academy of Arts, London,
30 June – 8 October 1995

This exhibition is made possible by a grant from

Cantor Fitzgerald

Masterpieces from
Swiss Private Collections

FROM MANET TO GAUGUIN

DOROTHY KOSINSKI, JOACHIM PISSARRO *and* MARYANNE STEVENS

ROYAL ACADEMY OF ARTS, LONDON, 1995
in association with
LUDION PRESS, GHENT

First published on the occasion of the exhibition
'FROM MANET TO GAUGUIN:
Masterpieces from Swiss Private Collections',
Royal Academy of Arts, London
30 June – 8 October 1995

The exhibition was conceived and initiated by

APOLLO

THE INTERNATIONAL MAGAZINE OF ART AND ANTIQUES
Established 1925
London, England

and organised by the Royal Academy of Arts

The Royal Academy of Arts is grateful to Her Majesty's Government
for its help in agreeing to indemnify the exhibition under the National
Heritage Act 1980, and to the Museums and Galleries Commission
for their help in arranging this indemnity.

Catalogue published in association with Ludion Press, Ghent
Catalogue design by Dooreman, Ghent
Typeset in Eric Gill's Joanna and Gill Sans by Ludion Press
Lithography by De Schutter, Antwerp
Printed in Belgium by Die Keure, Bruges

COVER: (front) Vincent van Gogh, Peasant Woman against a
Background of Wheat [cat. 72], late June 1890, Private Collection;
(back) Paul Cézanne, Médan: The Château and the Village
[cat. 6], c. 1885, Private Collection, Zurich

CONTENTS

SPONSOR'S PREFACE

Cantor Fitzgerald is proud to sponsor From Manet to Gauguin: Masterpieces from Swiss Private Collections *at the Royal Academy of Arts.*

Switzerland has established a remarkable tradition of private collecting. The Swiss were among the first outside France to appreciate Impressionist and Post-Impressionist art, and began collecting paintings by such masters as Manet, Monet, Van Gogh, Cézanne and Gauguin as early as the turn of the century. This tradition of connoisseurship remains just as strong today.

From Manet to Gauguin: Masterpieces from Swiss Private Collections *presents a number of great paintings that, until now, have never been accessible to the public. It is for that reason that Cantor Fitzgerald is especially pleased to be able to join the Royal Academy in presenting this exhibition. Cantor Fitzgerald is dedicated to supporting the arts and art scholarship, and is delighted to be able to offer audiences fresh revelations of the genius of the Impressionists and their successors.*

B. GERALD CANTOR
Chairman, Cantor Fitzgerald

PRESIDENT'S FOREWORD

In Switzerland, from around 1900, a small group of well-to-do businessmen and industrialists shrugged off the prevalent taste for contemporary German art, exemplified by Böcklin and Feuerbach, and adopted French Impressionism and Post-Impressionism as the new, radical manifestation of 'modern art'. Within two decades, major collections were assembled by such families as the Sulzers, Hahnlosers and Bühlers in Winterthur, the Browns in Baden, the Schulers in Zurich and the Müllers in Solothurn.

These collectors cultivated friendships with the more radical Swiss contemporary artists of the day – Ferdinand Hodler, Félix Vallotton, Cuno Amiet, Giovanni Giacometti and Carl Montag; visited exhibitions of contemporary French art in Basel, Zurich and Winterthur, and were in contact with Parisian dealers such as Vollard, Durand-Ruel and Bernheim-Jeune. They collected Cézannes, Gauguins and Van Goghs, as well as works by Sisley, Pissarro and Monet. Some even favoured the works of a younger generation of avant-garde artists, for example, Bonnard, Vuillard and Marquet, as well as those of the Symbolist Odilon Redon. Others, such as Müller, used their initial enthusiasm for late 19th-century French painting as a spring-board for the creation of major collections of 20th-century art, ranging from Picasso to Kandinsky. It was against this background that a pattern of collecting was established which, over the years, has continued to gather major works into private collections in Switzerland.

This exhibition focuses on the enduring taste in Switzerland for French Impressionist and Post-Impressionist works over the past ninety years. Works from the pioneering collections are shown here beside those from collections created more recently.

Many have assisted in the creation of this exhibition. First we owe a great debt of gratitude to the collectors themselves, who not only encouraged us in organising the exhibition and welcomed us into their homes, but who have also agreed so generously to lend their works. The research for the exhibition was initiated by Joachim Pissarro, and further pursued by Dorothy Kosinski and MaryAnne Stevens; together they undertook the selection of the works. Throughout they have been assisted by a large number of colleagues, and have enjoyed the support of successive Swiss Ambassadors in London and of Pro Helvetia in Zurich. We wish to express our thanks to our sponsor, Cantor Fitzgerald, and especially to Iris and B. Gerald Cantor, whose enthusiasm for the exhibition has ensured its realisation in London. Cantor Fitzgerald will also play a part in making possible the presentation of the exhibition when it travels on to Japan. We are delighted that it will be shown there in the Sezon Museum of Art, Tokyo, and in the Matsuzakaya Museum of Art, Nagoya. We are most grateful to The Tokyo Shimbun who are organising the Japanese tour with support from The Tokio Marine and Fire Insurance Co. Ltd.

The works of art in this exhibition usually hang in private homes, where they provide aesthetic pleasure and delight to their owners. We hope that during their brief stay at the Royal Academy, and later in Japan, they will afford similar delight to a wider public.

SIR PHILIP DOWSON CBE
President, Royal Academy of Arts

LENDERS TO THE EXHIBITION

BASEL, BEYELER COLLECTION

ERWIN AND RUTH BERNHEIM, HERRLIBERG

WERNER AND GABRIELLE MERZBACHER

SCHAFFHAUSEN, KUNSTMUSEUM

SOLOTHURN, KUNSTMUSEUM

RUDOLF STAECHELIN FAMILY FOUNDATION

ZURICH, FONDATION RAU POUR LE TIERS-MONDE

AND OTHER LENDERS WHO WISH TO REMAIN ANONYMOUS

ACKNOWLEDGEMENTS

We would like to extend our thanks to the advisers, lenders, directors and curators,
and also to the following people who have contributed to the organisation of the exhibition
and the preparation of the catalogue in many different ways:

Jania Aebi-Potocka

Doris Ammann

The late Thomas Ammann

Dr Walter Amstutz

Alex Apsis

E. A. Aufsesser

Fransziska Baetcke

Madame Jean-Paul Barbier-Müller

Dr Félix A. Baumann

Rolando Benedick

Nicolas Beurret

Ernst and Hildy Beyeler

Janet F. Briner

Annette Bühler

Dr Christian Bührle

Robert Clémentz

François Daulte

Walter Dräyer

Walter and Marianne Feilchenfeldt

Edouard and Thérèse Firino-Martell

Trude Fischer

Duchesse de la Force

Eric Franck

Madame Louis Franck

Matthias Frehner

The late Dr Christian Geelhaar

Bruno and Odette Giacometti

Léonard Gianadda

Patrick Goetelen

Dr Tina Grütter

François Gutzwiller

Prof. Dr Med. Paul and Magrit Hahnloser

Rodolphe Haller

Hans Hinz

Ay-Whang Hsia

Prof. Max Huggler

Walter Jöhr

Paul and Ellen Josefowitz

Prof. Philippe Junod

Dr André Kamber

Dr Thomas Kellein

Dan Klein

Dr Christian Klemm

Dr Rudolf Koella

Cyrille Koller

Jacqueline Krotoschin

Jan Krugier

Constantine Melas-Kryiazi

Dr and Madame Landoit-Sandoz

Claude Lapaire

Dr Hans A. Lüthy

Daniella Luxembourg

Elizabeth Markevitch

Irene Martin

Werner Merzbacher

Jean-Léonard de Meuron

Dr Franz Meyer

Chantal Michetti

Charles Moffett

Yozo Mori

The late Marguerite Motte

H. E. Franz E. Muheim

Alex Nathan

Dr Peter Nathan

Johannes Nathan

Philippe Natmann

Claudia Neugebauer

H. E. François Nordmann

Philippe Nordmann

Anne-Françoise Pelot

Dieter Pfister

Paul Pfister

Mr and Mrs Lionel Pissarro

Monsieur and Madame Christoph de Planta

Frau Dr Eva-Maria Preiswerk-Lösel

Simon de Pury

Dr Franz Reichenbach

Maria Reinshagen

Fernando Riba

Bernard and Chantal de Riedmatten

Dr Hortensia von Roda

James Roundell

Peter Schälchli

Dr Katharina Schmidt

Dr Dieter Schwarz

Albert Skira

Mr and Mrs Ruedi Staechelin

Adolphe Stein

Verena Steiner-Jäggli

Romy Storrer

Michel Strauss

Dr Hans Christian von Tavel

Marina G. Thouin

Kurt Tiegermann

Victor R. Tiegermann

Louis Trujillo

Donald Vallotton

Philippe Vallotton

Rodolphe Vallotton de Veley

Daniel Varenne

Claire Vauthier-Neyroud

Carlo von Castelberg

Lic. iur. Leonard J. Toenz

Dr Roland Wäspi

Gerard and Valerie Wertheimer

David and Fatma Turkkan Wille

Dr and Mrs Jörg Wille

Ully Wille

Renate Woudhuysen

Dr Jörg Zutter

This exhibition has been researched by
JOACHIM PISSARRO
with the assistance of
CLAIRE DURAND-RUEL SNOELLAERTS

Selected and organised by
JOACHIM PISSARRO, DOROTHY KOSINSKI *and*
MARYANNE STEVENS
Bibliography compiled by FRANZISKA BAETCKE

Exhibition Coordinators
EMELINE MAX
SUSAN THOMPSON

Exhibition Research Assistants
CORINNE WELLESLEY *and* KATIE KLITGAARD

Editorial Coordinator
JANE MARTINEAU

Photographic Coordinator
MIRANDA BENNION

EDITORIAL NOTE

Dimensions are given in centimetres to the nearest 0.5 cm; height precedes width.

The following abbreviations are used in the catalogue section:

CÉZANNE

V: *Lionello Venturi,* Cézanne: Son art, son œuvre
(Paris 1936)

DEGAS

L: *Paul-André Lemoisne,* Degas et son œuvre,
*4 vols. (Paris 1946–9); reprinted with a supplement by Philippe Brame
and Theodore Reff (New York and London 1984)*

GAUGUIN

W: *Georges Wildenstein,* Gauguin,
ed. Raymond Cogniat and Daniel Wildenstein (Paris 1964)

VAN GOGH

F: *J. B. de la Faille,* The Works of Vincent van Gogh: His Paintings and Drawings
(New York 1970)

MANET

RW: *Denis Rouart and Daniel Wildenstein,* Edouard Manet, Catalogue raisonné,
2 vols. (Lausanne and Paris 1974)

MONET

W: *Georges Wildenstein,* Claude Monet: Biographie et catalogue raisonné,
5 vols. (Lausanne and Paris 1974, 1979, 1979, 1985, 1991)

PISSARRO

PV: *Ludovic Pissarro and Lionello Venturi,* Camille Pissarro: Son art, son œuvre,
2 vols. (Paris 1938)

RENOIR

D: *François Daulte,* Auguste Renoir: Catalogue raisonné de l'œuvre peint
(Lausanne 1971)

SISLEY

D: *François Daulte,* Alfred Sisley: Catalogue raisonné de l'œuvre peint
(Lausanne 1959)

TOULOUSE-LAUTREC

DP: *M. G. Dortu,* Toulouse-Lautrec et son œuvre,
6 vols. (New York 1971)

fig.1   *Ernst Würtenberger, Board of the Kunstverein,*
Winterthur, 1915. Kunstmuseum Winterthur.
Left to right: Richard Bühler, Robert Rittmeyer (standing),
Georg Reinhart, Paul Fink (curator of the Kunstverein),
Arthur Hahnloser (seated, foreground right),
Hans Sulzer (standing, far right).

French Impressionism and Post-Impressionism:
THE ESTABLISHMENT
OF A NEW TASTE IN SWITZERLAND

Dorothy Kosinski
Joachim Pissarro
MaryAnne Stevens

This exhibition is concerned with the reception of French Impressionism and Post-Impressionism by private collectors in Switzerland after 1900. Around the turn of the century, enthusiastic Swiss amateurs redefined the meaning of the term 'modern art'. Rather than equating it with academic German and Swiss art epitomised in the work of Böcklin, 'modern art' came to mean contemporary, and near contemporary French avant-garde art, namely the work of the Impressionists and Post-Impressionists. The impact of such a shift in definition is found in the pioneer collections made between *c.*1905 and the outbreak of World War I. Here, enthusiasm for Cézanne, Pissarro, Gauguin and Van Gogh was complemented by a taste for such avant-garde Swiss artists as Ferdinand Hodler, Cuno Amiet, Giovanni Giacometti and Félix Vallotton, and pursued even further with French artists of the younger genera-tion such as Bonnard, Vuillard, Marquet, Manguin and Matisse. Some of these early collectors continued to update the definition of 'modern art', carrying their col-lecting into subsequent manifestations of modern art. To have studied this evolution could have provided one basis for an exhibition. This exhibition reviews the con-tinuation of that initial enthusiasm for Impressionism and Post-Impressionism. To be sure, different genera-tions of collectors have been influenced by different factors. Thus, collections made between 1930 and 1950 were inevitably informed by the economic crash of 1929, the arrival of émigré collectors and dealers in the 1930s and the singularity of the Swiss art market during World War II. In the post-war years, the pattern of taste for this art reflects the establishment of a buoyant and open art market, with its confirmation of Impressionism and Post-Impressionism as the pioneering styles of modern art.

The conjunction of particular forces at specific moments has suggested that patterns of taste can be identified within each phase in the history of collecting Impressionism and Post-Impressionism in Switzerland. However, an element of idiosyncrasy tends to inform each collector's choice of artist and individual works, and the task is not made easier given the fact that many collectors wish to remain anonymous. Considerable information has been published on the pioneer collec-tions, but the history of those created even as early as the 1930s is still relatively inaccessible.

The small group of collectors in Switzerland who had learnt of the existence of French Impressionism and Post-Impressionism initiated a major shift in taste which was to have important consequences for the cultural history of Switzerland. The story is one of enthusiasm for an art which, before 1900, had been deemed by most citizens of Switzerland as dangerously revolutionary and a threat to national and cultural identity.

While the acceptance of Impressionism in America, Germany, Russia and France has been recorded, in Switzerland it has generally escaped the attention of scholars. There are several reasons for this.

Whereas the countries surrounding Switzerland had established traditions of patronage and collecting, until the beginning of the 20th century neither tradition was significantly present in Switzerland. There was one notable exception: Basilius Amerbach and a small group of enlightened collectors in late 16th-century Basel.[1] Amerbach died in 1591 leaving a sub-stantial collection, including a numismatic collection, fifty paintings, of which fifteen were by Holbein the Younger, and an extremely important group of drawings (50 by Holbein the Elder, 12 by Baldung Grien, 115 by Urs Graf, 70 by Niklaus Manuel Deutsch, and about 240 by Holbein the Younger). Thanks to the tenacity of Amerbach's heirs and the public spirit of the citizens of Basel, the Amerbach collection avoided the fate of most non-princely collections and was not dispersed on the market. In the 1630s, the Earl of Arundel made a substantial offer for part of the drawings collection; this and all subsequent offers were turned down, and in 1661 Amerbach's descendants sold the collection to the City of Basel, thus turning it into the first public museum in Europe.

Swiss collectors have always valued privacy, and have not publicised their achievement as a 'nation'. The very idea of a nation is foreign to the Swiss: it is difficult for a British, French or German person to imagine that a resident of Glarus or St Gallen can consider someone from Geneva, Lausanne or Lugano, if not a foreigner, at least a very different type of Swiss citizen. This fragmentation of the Swiss cultural map has hindered the formation of a Swiss cultural identity.

Equally important is the fact that most collections in Switzerland have remained distinctly private. Hence it has been difficult to assess the progress of its taste for modern French art. Elsewhere in Europe, when an important Impressionist work entered a museum, the acquisition has been commented upon by critics and publicised in the media. By contrast, should a private collector in a remote canton of Switzerland acquire a Cézanne, it could remain unrecorded, sometimes for generations.

The history of Swiss collecting both in the pioneering phase before World War I and in more recent decades invites us to examine why and how Switzerland played so significant a role in promoting the taste for Modernism. Two qualities are common to Swiss collectors both past and present: discretion and understatement. The pioneers in the early decades of the century tended to work independently of the major institutions; unlike their American counterparts, they generally publicised their collections either collectively, as in the loans committed to the Winterthur Kunstmuseum in 1917 which enabled the museum to install the first 'Franzosensaal' in Switzerland, or in small, limited-edition catalogues, such as that published by Georg Reinhart of his collection in 1922.

The Swiss fiscal system has acted sympathetically towards collectors and their descendants. Inheritance tax only has to be paid if a work of art is sold. Thus the State encouraged private individuals to preserve their cultural heritage with, for example, the Hahnloser collection passing down through three generations and the Brown collection being entrusted to a foundation only on the death of the last survivor of the second generation.

While Swiss citizens are isolated from one other, Switzerland, through its position at the heart of Europe, has been exposed to a number of external influences. The gradual conquest by Impressionism was achieved in the face of the prevalent taste for German and Swiss academic art. More remarkably, French Impressionism was introduced into Switzerland through its German-speaking community; the earliest collectors of Impressionism in Switzerland were from Basel, Winterthur and Zurich, and not from French-speaking Geneva or Lausanne. Moreover, the critics and museum professionals with the greatest impact on German-Swiss collectors were more often German than French. Only later did the French-speaking regions of Switzerland share this interest in French Impressionism, notably after Bernheim-Jeune opened a branch of its gallery in Lausanne in 1913. This can be explained by various economic and cultural factors. By the end of the 19th century the north-eastern, German-speaking part of Switzerland lying between Bern and St Gallen had experienced rapid economic growth based upon steel, textiles and chemicals. As the infrastructure of the

modern Swiss economy was being established, large individual fortunes were being made. The new rich industrialists felt a natural affinity for all innovations. In this they were supported by the example of a determined group of industrialists and museum directors in Germany, notably the director of the Nationalgalerie in Berlin, Hugo von Tschudi (himself Swiss in origin).

THE INSTITUTIONAL FRAMEWORK FOR THE NEW TASTE

The conversion of Swiss collectors to Impressionism did not occur suddenly. Many of the pioneer collectors had initially followed the taste of the last decades of the 19th century for academic German or Swiss art, epitomised by the art of Arnold Böcklin. But even here, the will to collect seems not to have been so strongly developed, as Böcklin himself stated in a letter of 1881 written in Florence to his friend and colleague, Frank Buchser:

> … as I see things at the moment, it seems to me unlikely that art will ever come to yield any fruit in Switzerland – in spite of the best exhibitions which one can see with good light there. I think that the interest in art is much too limited there. This would not matter so much if Switzerland were a large country. Indeed, amidst many millions of people, you would always find a sufficient number of those for whom art and the possession of works of art is a need; at home, however, these few people are soon counted up.[2]

Böcklin's conclusion as regards Switzerland was based on his experience of other European countries where he found many institutions which could show his works to an art-loving public: he believed that he could find no equivalent institutions in Switzerland.

Böcklin's judgement was too harsh, for institutions supporting contemporary art had been in existence in Switzerland since the 1840s.[3] These were the Schweizerische Kunstvereine, provincial art associations who pledged allegiance either to their canton or, in some cases, to their town. The Kunstvereine of Winterthur and Zurich were regularly in competition with each other. The function of the Kunstvereine was to hold temporary exhibitions, 'Turnus-Ausstellungen', which would bring contemporary art to the Swiss public [fig. 2]. Indeed, Kunstvereine played a crucial role in establishing a direct market link between artists and the Swiss public. Their exhibitions were principally held for local artists, although there were a few exceptions: artists from Germany were occasionally invited, as well as some Swiss expatriates such as Grob, J.G. Steffan and A. Stäbli. Despite their relatively limited scope, these

fig. 2 *Turnus-Ausstellung poster, 1906.*

shows created a base for the revolution of taste which was to take place in Switzerland over the following decades. The exhibitions offered an unprecedented opportunity for the public to inform itself of artistic developments outside Switzerland; and the Kunstvereine, since they were relatively new, tended to be tolerant of academic artists as well as their more radical counterparts. Such catholic taste was almost without precedent elsewhere in Europe where academic and more radical art was usually shown in separate venues.

This liberal acceptance of the diversity of contemporary art was reflected in collections being formed at that time. A good case in point is the La Roche-Ringwald collection formed in Basel in the last decades of the 19th century. The core of the collection consisted of seven Böcklins, surrounded by paintings by Anker, Zünd, Bucher – 'academic' Swiss artists who had achieved great fame by the end of the century. Much more surprising was the presence in the collection of Hodler. It also included works by German academic artists such as Von Max, Von Lenbach and Zimmermann, as well as some by their fellow compatriots, the Realist Wilhelm Leibl and the Impressionist Max Liebermann, both of whom were *personae non gratae* among the official circles of the German court.

While the La Roche-Ringwald collection offered a precedent for the introduction of modern art into Switzerland after 1900, an institutional innovation equal in importance to the Kunstvereine occurred in 1894 with the creation of the Verein für bildende Kunst. Unlike the Kunstvereine, the Verein für bildende Kunst was founded to ensure the establishment of a permanent institution, the Zurich Künstlerhaus, in 1895, whose exhibition policies were to be even more liberal and international than those of the Turnus-Austellungen. The Zurich Künstlerhaus was founded at the home of a Zurich collector, Gustav Henneberg, whose interest lay in Swiss and German academic art; a selection from his private collection was shown in nearby premises at its inaugural exhibition in 1895. Shortly afterwards, forty-nine artists working in Switzerland and abroad were asked to lend to one of the first museums to organise temporary exhibitions in Switzerland.[4] With the exception of Giovanni Segantini, Max Liebermann and Wilhelm Leibl, all the invited artists were of an academic persuasion: among the Swiss were Weckesser, Anker, Stückelberger and Zünd; among the foreigners were the German Von Lenbach and the French Auguste Truphème and Jobbe-Duval. This set a precedent for exhibiting the work of foreign avant-garde artists in Switzerland.

In 1897 the Zurich Kunstgesellschaft stated that it could 'no longer afford not to show French art'.[5]

It contacted the French dealers, Chaîne & Simonson, and the first exhibition of contemporary French art took place in Zurich in 1897. It contained eighty works by forty-two artists who normally exhibited either with the Société Nationale des Beaux-Arts or the Société des Artistes français in Paris. While the exhibition excluded the more radical members of the French avant-garde, it opened the eyes of the Swiss to French art. The shock of this art was evident in a remark made by Hermann Clausen, a Zurich art critic, to Chaîne & Simonson: 'Everything is new to them; they are afraid of voicing their opinions, not wishing to find fault with themselves.'[6] Yet, it is worth noting that, while Switzerland was opening its doors to more conventional contemporary French art, the French public was only beginning to be aware of such names as Cézanne, Van Gogh and Gauguin through the efforts of the dealer Ambroise Vollard who arranged monographic exhibitions of their work in 1895, 1896 and 1897 respectively. Only a few years after these exhibitions their names also became known in Switzerland.

One further event of critical importance in the evolution of Swiss taste was the celebration of the 70th birthday of Switzerland's most important artist, Arnold Böcklin, which involved a major exhibition at the Basel Kunsthalle. The exhibition was an outstanding success, attracting an unprecedented 30,000 visitors from both Switzerland and Germany. The show also provided the occasion for Heinrich Wölfflin, then Professor of Art History at the University of Basel, to outline in a lecture a new critical framework for modern art which would shape the reception of a more radical avant-garde. In writing of the 'profundity of Böcklin's interior creation', Wölfflin saw that Böcklin's art was abandoning traditional models and oscillating between realism and idealism. Although Wölfflin cannot be suspected of showing any sympathy towards Impressionism or more recent avant-garde movements, he defined the characteristics of Böcklin's art through a vocabulary which could have been applied to some aspects of Impressionism and certainly to Symbolism.[7] As early as 1883, the French critic Jules Laforgue, who was largely responsible for introducing Impressionism to the German-speaking world by organising an exhibition of Impressionist works for the Gurlitt Gallery in Berlin, defined the characteristics of Impressionism as a fusion of subject and object – or to put it in Wölfflinian terms, between the real and the 'interior profundity' of the artist: '… object and subject [nature and the artist] are … irretrievably in motion, incapable of being understood and understanding at the same time. In the flashes of identity between subject and object lies the nature of genius.'[8] In 1892, only a few years before Wölfflin's lecture on Böcklin, the

French poet and critic Albert Aurier had characterised Van Gogh's art in very similar terms, measuring the 'degrees of the artist's passive sincerity before nature',[9] or, in other words, gauging the 'inner profundity' of the artist's sensitivity in response to nature.

'Profundity', 'sincerity', 'abandon of traditional models', 'novelty', 'originality' – all these terms, whether used by Wölfflin, Laforgue or Aurier, provided a way of describing a new spirit in painting which had departed from the traditionally accepted canons of excellence. Wölfflin's application of these terms indicated that the situation was ripe in Switzerland for the introduction of Impressionism. This is implicit in the words of the president of the Basler Kunstverein in 1896 when he announced an exhibition devoted to the Munich Secession: 'To be modern, such is the motto at the end of the 19th century.'[10]

Publications offering a new interpretation or an historical framework for Impressionism played an important role, too, in establishing a taste for French art in Switzerland. Richard Muther's *Geschichte der Malerei im XIX. Jahrhundert*, published in Munich in 1893, for example, discussed Impressionism in its last chapter under the appropriately combative title 'Schlusswort im grossen Befreiungskampf der modernen Kunst'.

Julius Meier-Graefe's *Entwicklungsgeschichte der modernen Kunst* (Stuttgart 1904), which provided a critico-historical structure for French Impressionism, was probably even more influential [fig.3]. Meier-Graefe argued that French Impressionism was the latest, and most decisive, manifestation of a historical tradition in the visual arts that he called 'das Malerische' ('the painterly'). He insisted on applying formal analysis to works of art, which brought its own moral imperative – rather than interpreting them in terms of biography or psychology. He claimed that there is an aesthetic quality common to all great art, and challenged the history of art based on national characteristics initially elaborated by the French philosopher Hippolyte Taine. The book gave rise to a variety of responses: it was popular with the innovative collectors, but elicited harsh criticism, often tinged with nationalistic or racist overtones, from conservatives. These critics objected to his formal critical methods, and especially to his linking of the tradition of great art with a notion of moral probity. Their strident criticism sometimes took the form of personal attacks: they claimed that Meier-Graefe was a dealer interested only in his own financial advancement, they remarked that he was Jewish and suggested that he was unpatriotic. The co-opting of Impressionism as a subject in politico-social debates focused on nationality or race was to become

prevalent both in Germany and in Switzerland.[11]

The importance of the Swiss avant-garde artists in discovering and publicising the works of French Impressionists was also crucial. At the second Berlin Secession, held in 1900, Hodler exhibited beside Liebermann, Pissarro, Renoir and Vuillard. Three years later, at the same organisation, he appeared beside Cézanne, Gauguin, Van Gogh, Manet, Monet, Pissarro, Toulouse-Lautrec and Vuillard. The following year, at the 19th Viennese Secession, he was hung alongside Hans von Marées, Edvard Munch and the Finnish artist Axel Gallen. It was the intention of this Secession to reveal to the public 'the latest phase of artistic development'.[12] Other contemporary artists such as Cuno Amiet, Giovanni Giacometti, Félix Vallotton and, after his move to Paris in 1903, Carl Montag, also exhibited in Europe and acted as mediators of the new French art.

Their role was highlighted in 1906 by the secretary of the Zurich Kunstgesellschaft: 'In Zurich and in Switzerland, we only know the works of these [i.e. French avant-garde] artists through the works of Amiet and [Giovanni] Giacometti ... We would wish to see the originals with our own eyes: the real Frenchmen! Such has been our wish for a long time; this is our deepest wish and that of our artists.'[13] This sentiment was echoed in a review of the 1908 Van Gogh exhibition (the first major retrospective show to be held in Europe) published in the *Neue Züricher Zeitung*: 'Imagine how he [Van Gogh] would have surprised us, even more, stunned us, had it not been for Amiet and [Giovanni] Giacometti, who had already long since accustomed us to a scale of pure and violent colours [*Farbklänge*] ... They initiated us into Van Gogh.'[14]

Amiet's vibrant palette and aggressive brushstrokes seem to have been the key to Swiss collectors' positive response to the Van Gogh exhibition at the Künstlerhaus Zurich in 1908. His strong colouristic expressionism offered a link to the Post-Impressionists and made a bridge to Fauvism and Expressionism, and his impact on the taste of his student Gertrud Dübi-Müller was significant. Amiet, as presented in Oskar Miller's collection, was also a revelation for her brother Josef Müller, who, on Amiet's advice purchased in 1914 Renoir's *Bulgarian Blouse*. Amiet himself collected works by the Impressionists, including those of Pissarro.

Richard Kisling's collection offered a survey of modern Swiss painting, including works by Hodler, Amiet and both Giovanni and Augusto Giacometti, but also Blanchet, Vallet, Vautier, Trachsel, Auberjonois, Berger, R. Théoph. Robert and Muret. Kisling purchased Van Gogh's *Young Girl Standing against a Background of Wheat* (1890; F.788) directly from the exhibi-

fig.3 *Frontispiece of* Widmungen zu seinem sechzigsten Geburstage, *1927. Photograph of Julius Meier-Graefe.*

fig.4 *Vincent van Gogh, Mme Roulin and her Baby, 1888. Philadelphia Museum of Art (formerly Meyer-Fierz collection)*

fig.5 *Vincent van Gogh, Straw Roofs near Auvers, 1890. Kunsthaus Zurich, Bequest Dr Hans Schuler, 1920.*

fig.6 *Exhibition of Swiss art, 1897, hung in the Town Hall, Winterthur.*

fig.7 *View of the Ausstellung von Kunstwerken aus Winterthurer Privatbesitz (Winterthur Private Collections), 1911, showing works by Bonnard, Marquet and Vallotton.*

tion, and later *Two Children* (1890; F.784); Fritz Meyer-Fierz and Hans Schuler also bought works from the Van Gogh exhibition [figs.4, 5].

Two major exhibitions laid the foundations for the reception of Impressionism in Switzerland. In 1906, Léonce Bénédite, Conservateur of the Musée National du Luxembourg (the French national museum of modern art), organised for the Basel Kunsthalle an exhibition entitled Exposition d'Art Français.[15] Two years later, an Impressionist exhibition was organised by the Zurich Künstlerhaus. The commissaires for this exhibition were two artists, Hans Sturzenegger and Ernst Würtzerger, and the collector Richard Kisling, who in the spring of 1908 had visited Paul Durand-Ruel's gallery in Paris. The core of the exhibition was formed from the collection of a Swiss resident of Frankfurt, Ottilie Röderstein. Having agreed to lend her collection, she proposed that Wilhelm Uhde, the German critic-collector resident in Paris, should select the rest of the exhibition. Uhde contacted Durand-Ruel and Bernheim-Jeune, the two foremost Parisian dealers specialising in French Impressionism, and negotiated the loans of over a hundred works by Impressionist and Post-Impressionist artists. The exhibition provoked a great debate in Zurich: the architect Alexander von Senger, for instance, was adamantly dismissive of what he regarded as an invasion of Switzerland by decadent French art; while others, such as Ernst Bovet, president of the periodical *Wissen und Leben*, and influential citizens such as Hans Schuler, were ardent defenders of the new French tendencies. The impact of these two exhibitions in Basel and Zurich was soon felt, and collectors began to amass remarkable works by French Impressionists and particularly by Post-Impressionists.

Temporary exhibitions continued to play an influential role in the support of these collections and the formation of new ones. The 1911 exhibition organised by the Kunstverein Winterthur, Ausstellung von Kunstwerken aus Winterthurer Privatbesitz, can be regarded both as the product of and a catalyst for renewed collecting activities in Winterthur. In part the exhibition reflected the collecting pattern of earlier Kunstverein exhibitions. Thus the more conventional Swiss artists such as Stäbli, Graff and Koller were shown alongside Hodler, Amiet, Segantini, Vallotton and Giacometti, as well as French Modernists, including Renoir, Bonnard, Marquet and Manguin. Indeed such was the strength of the Winterthur collections that fifty out of some two hundred works in the exhibition were lent by local collectors. The exhibition also provided established and new collectors with the opportunity to purchase works off the walls, and by the close of the show some fifty had entered private hands.

It had taken less than twenty years, from 1897, the year of the first exhibition in Switzerland dedicated to French Salon painting, to around 1910, for 'modern art' to form a dominant part of Swiss private collections [figs.6, 7]. Soon Switzerland became known as a centre of important new collections of modern art. In the exhibition, Französische Bilder aus der Schweiz, held in Stuttgart in 1913, Impressionism was represented by thirty-nine paintings, of which a third came from private collections in Winterthur and Baden. These loans had been negotiated by Carl Montag, the adviser to several of the collectors.

As elsewhere in Europe, modern art received a mixed reception in Switzerland. The regular visitors to the Turnus-Ausstellungen, as well as the general public, accustomed as they were to more traditional art, did not react favourably to the new, foreign art. There was a need to bridge the critical gap between collectors and the public. Artists, museum professionals, art dealers, critics and journalists came to play an essential role.

Carl Montag (1880–1956), a native of Winterthur, abandoned painting a few years after arriving in Paris in 1903. Thereafter his role was that of dealer or

adviser. Montag guided the formation of the collection of Sidney and Jenny Brown-Sulzer in Baden, and advised Hans Mettler in St Gallen, Willy Russ-Suchard in Neuchâtel and Emil Staub-Terlinden in Männedorf, as well as, to a lesser extent, the Hahnlosers, Bühlers and Reinharts in Winterthur. Not only was he the conduit between collector and artist, and between collector and dealer or gallery, but also the guiding force behind an astounding number of exhibitions between 1913 and 1949. These included survey exhibitions of French painting staged in Zurich in 1913, Winterthur in 1916, Basel in 1917 and Geneva in 1918, and important monographic shows devoted to Redon (Winterthur, 1919), Picasso (Zurich, 1932), Léger (Zurich, 1933) and Gris (Zurich, 1933). Montag also helped to present important Swiss collections abroad: in 1913 in Stuttgart, at the Französische Bilder aus der Schweiz exhibition, and in 1938, at the Galerie de la Gazette des Beaux-Arts in Paris, Peinture française du XIXe siècle dans les collections privées suisses.[16]

The Kunsthalle Basel was responsible in the 1920s for important exhibitions of Impressionism, continuing a tradition established in the first Impressionist exhibitions of 1906 and 1908 whereby between a quarter and a third of the works displayed were available for purchase. This policy had offered a huge incentive to the Swiss public not only to discover this new art, but also to possess it. This was only possible through the collaboration of the dealers, most notably the Parisians Ambroise Vollard, Bernheim-Jeune and Paul Durand-Ruel; Paul Cassirer, who represented Durand-Ruel in Berlin; and Thannhauser in Munich. They all sent works from their stock for exhibition and for sale. They also established relationships with dealers in Switzerland: Vollard with Wolfensberger and Bernheim-Jeune with Tanner in Zurich; Bernheim-Jeune with Vallotton in Lausanne, and Thannhauser with Rosengart in Lucerne. In addition, independent dealers also emerged, such as Neupert in Zurich and Moos in Geneva. The growth of exhibition organisations and the expansion of private collecting brought a further change in Switzerland: the direction of museums moved from the control of local amateurs or artists and became, in the case of the Zurich Künstlerhaus (renamed the Kunsthaus in 1909) and the Basel Kunstmuseum, the domain of professional art historians.

In 1913 an exhibition entitled Französische Kunst was held in Zurich. It provided the Swiss public with its first opportunity to gauge the interrelationship between Swiss contemporary painting and French Impressionism. Wilhelm Wartmann, director of the Kunsthaus, explained to Bernheim-Jeune, one of the most important lenders, that the exhibition had been 'conçue et réalisée d'après un plan médité et équilibré'.[17] In the same year, another exhibition, entitled Französische Meister was held in Basel. This offered a more historical perspective on the successive phases in the history of contemporary art. Three years later, in 1916, the Kunstverein in Winterthur mounted its own exhibition of Französische Malerei [fig.8–9]. This included approximately two hundred works of which about a quarter came from Winterthur from the collections of Brown, Bühler, Hahnloser, Georg Reinhart and Sulzer. And in 1917, in the middle of World War I, the Zurich Kunsthaus staged two exhibitions: Französische Kunst and Deutsche Ausstellung. With the war raging around them, the Swiss were acutely aware of their neutrality and the cultural implications of such a stance. Carl Montag was invited by the French Minister of Foreign Affairs to select a representative display of French art which would promote French art and culture in neutral Switzerland. Over 20,000 people visited the French exhibition. Fewer than 10,000 visited the parallel German Exhibition.

While major group exhibitions of Impressionist and Post-Impressionist works continued to be held in Switzerland, these were increasingly interspersed with one-man exhibitions such as that of Hodler at the Zurich Kunsthaus in 1917, and of Odilon Redon at the Kunstmuseum Winterthur two years later. [JP]

figs.8-9 *Ausstellung Französischer Malerei (French Painting exhibition), Kunstmuseum Winterthur, 1916. Left: French Impressionists from the collections of Emil Staub-Terlinden, Georg Reinhart, Hans Schuler, Sidney Brown, Arthur and Hedy Hahnloser, Hans Reinhart; right: room of French Impressionists.*

fig.10 *Richard Bühler.*

fig.11 *Villa Tössertobel, Winterthur, designed by Rittmeyer and Furrer (1907) for Georg Reinhart. The gardens were designed by the same architects and laid out in 1908.*

From the turn of the century to 1918 the major Swiss collections of Impressionism and Post-Impressionism were concentrated in a few cities and industrial centres in north-eastern Switzerland: Winterthur, Baden, Zurich, St Gallen, Solothurn and Basel. The most important collectors in Winterthur were the ophthalmologist Arthur Hahnloser-Bühler and his wife, Hedy; Arthur's brother Emil Hahnloser (1874–1940); the textile magnate Richard Bühler (Mrs Hahnloser's cousin) and his brother Hermann Bühler (1870–1926); the electrical engineer Sidney Brown (1865–1941) and Jenny Brown-Sulzer (1871–1968) who settled in Baden, and Jenny's brother Hans Sulzer (1876–1959), a member of the board of Sulzer Co. and Swiss ambassador to Washington in 1917–19; the Reinhart family – Theodor Reinhart (1849–1919), head of the trading company Volkart, himself a collector of Swiss and German art, and his sons Georg (1877–1955), Hans, Werner and Oskar (1885–1965); and the industrialist Heinrich Wolfer (1882–1969). In St Gallen there was the textile magnate Hans Mettler (1876–1945), whose wife was a cousin of Hedy Hahnloser-Bühler. In Zurich the major collectors included Hans Schuler (1869–1920) – yet another cousin of Hedy Hahnloser; Fritz Meyer-Fierz (1847–1917) and Richard Kisling (1862–1917); and in Männedorf, Emil Staub-Terlinden. In Solothurn the most important figures were Oskar Miller (1867–1934), although his collection was devoted to Swiss modern masters, Gertrud Dübi-Müller (1888–1980) and her brother, the paper manufacturer Josef Müller (1887–1977); in Basel, Rudolf Staechelin (1881–1946), and in Neuchâtel, Willy Russ-Suchard. With the exception of Dr Hahnloser, all the collectors were successful industrialists or businessmen.

These collectors made the dramatic switch away from the prevalent taste for German art to French painting, in particular to Impressionism and Post-Impressionism. This shift in taste was also linked to a growing appreciation for the modern Swiss masters, including Ferdinand Hodler, Cuno Amiet and Giovanni Giacometti. These artists, and others, such as Carl Montag, played an active role in promoting French art.

The Swiss collections of modern French art were formed at an astonishing speed. Oskar Miller in Solothurn, for example, had started his collection in 1896, as had Sidney and Jenny Brown-Sulzer of Winterthur and Baden. Significantly, the Browns only bought a Boudin and a Trouillebert in that year;[18] like their fellow collectors in Winterthur, they did not start seriously to collect Impressionists and Post-Impressionists until they bought a Cézanne still-life from Vollard in 1908. It was thus in the years around 1908 that the pioneering collections were formed: those of Josef and his sister Gertrud Müller in Solothurn; Arthur and Hedy Hahnloser-Bühler and Richard Bühler in Winterthur, Hans Mettler in St Gallen, and Richard Kisling, Fritz Meyer-Fierz and Hans Schuler in Zurich. These were followed by a younger generation of collectors, such as Georg Reinhart (who started in 1911) and his brother Oskar, who only began in earnest after World War I.

In 1907 the Hahnlosers made their first purchase, Hodler's *Das Kirschbäumlein* of 1905, but within two years Félix Vallotton could describe the Hahnlosers' Villa Flora in Winterthur as a 'veritable museum', devoted – at this time – primarily to Swiss artists.[19] Georg Reinhart began collecting in 1904, only concentrating on Impressionist works from 1911; in 1922 he was able to celebrate his collection with a private publication including 176 items. The speed with which Impressionism came to dominate these newly formed collections is perhaps most evident in Winterthur, where by 1907 the board of the Kunstverein was taken over by a dynamic group of patrons of a younger generation that included the architect Robert Rittmeyer [fig.11], Georg Reinhart, Richard Bühler, Arthur Hahnloser and Hans Sulzer. Reinhart, Hahnloser, Sulzer and Bühler [fig.10] all became major collectors, the last named becoming chairman of the board in 1912 [fig.1].[20] Equally significant is the fact that Rittmeyer's new museum, built in a classical Jugendstil which echoed the new aesthetic taste, was completed in 1916, during World War I [fig.27]! In 1919 the Kunstmuseum Winterthur was the first museum to stage an exhibition of the work of Odilon Redon. In 1935, the museum's exhibition of over eighty works by Renoir was drawn exclusively from local collections.[21] The same concentration and dynamism also characterised the formation of Hans Mettler's collection in St Gallen. Starting in 1915 with the purchase of a major Hodler landscape, the collection was formed within the next fourteen years, crowned with the purchase of Cézanne's *Une Baignade* (Private Collection, USA). In Basel, in a period of fifteen years, Rudolf Staechelin assembled a collection of works by Swiss modern artists, by French Impressionists [see cat.3, 14, 26, 50], and also masterworks by Matisse and Picasso.

Thus, when Pierre Courthion's two-part, lavishly illustrated article, 'L'Art français dans les collections privées en Suisse', appeared in 1926, he enthusiastically reported on his visits to various collections, including those of Oskar Reinhart, Sidney and Jenny Brown, Emil Staub, Georg Reinhart, Emil Hahnloser, Alwin Schmid (a small collection essentially devoted to the work of Corot, Watteau and Boudin), Richard Bühler and

fig.12 *Sidney and Jenny Brown with their children, c. 1906.*

fig.13 *Sidney Brown (seated) and Dr Georges Viau,*
in Viau's Paris apartment, c. 1910.

Arthur Hahnloser: 'Imagine a living history of French art, composed in a small corner of Switzerland, a garden with some of the most beautiful flowers of our painting, an assemblage of great beauty in a sympathetic environment – calm and welcoming. Here are the painters and most specifically those of the 19th century.'[22]

THE COLLECTORS – FOUR CASE STUDIES

The Sidney Brown and Jenny Brown-Sulzer collection (today the Langmatt Stiftung, Baden), assembled essentially between 1908 and 1919, concentrated on works by Renoir, Cézanne and Pissarro [fig. 12]. Although they bought two French works in 1896, their collection was centred around such German artists as Franz von Stuck, Julius Exter, Gotthardt Kühl and Ludwig Herevich [fig. 14]. It was only with the chance purchase of a Cézanne in Paris in 1908 that the character of the collection began to change rapidly. Still-lifes and landscapes predominated, the Browns favouring small-scale works of restrained taste [fig. 15]. The Swiss artist Carl Montag energetically guided the Browns' collecting over many years. He introduced the Browns to the Parisian collector and dentist Georges Viau (c. 1855–1939) from whom they bought a large number of pictures [fig. 13]. Viau had befriended many of the Impressionist artists, welcoming them to his apartment on the Boulevard Haussmann; he made his own vast collection, with works by all the major figures. Certain artists were well represented: more than nineteen paintings by Pissarro, at least twelve works by Sisley, fifteen by Renoir, as well as countless works on paper. Viau's first collection was dispersed at auction and in private sales between 1907 and 1909.[23] The Brown collection, as might be expected, reflected Viau's personal taste. It certainly profited from Viau's friendships in the Impressionist circle.

The Browns also purchased works from the major dealers, especially those in Paris (Ambroise Vollard, Paul Durand-Ruel, Georges Bernheim, Bernheim-Jeune, Druet), in Switzerland (Galerie Moos in Geneva, Georg Tanner and Galerie Neupert in Zurich) and in Germany (Paul Cassirer and Galerie Heinemann in Berlin). Yet, despite the guidance of dealers and advisers, a distinct personal taste and a real understanding of French Impressionism is discernible. There are significant works by Boudin, Pissarro, Renoir and Cézanne, Renoir being particularly well represented by landscapes and figures, flower pieces and still-lifes, sketches and highly finished works, ranging in date from 1874 to 1915.[24] Individual purchases also reveal the adventurousness and confidence of the collectors. Cézanne's *Pêches et carafe sur nappe* [fig. 16], purchased from Vollard on the advice of the Russian collector Sergey Shchukin in 1908 – one of the first works by the artist to enter Switzerland – is a challenging composition, juxtaposing the heavy fruit with daring passages of thin, loosely applied paint, which might suggest that it was unfinished. Another noteworthy acquisition was that in 1910 of Monet's *Débâcle de la Seine* (1893): a severe vision of winter with a composition reduced to broad horizontal bands. However, given that they were offered at the same time Monet's *Falaises à Etretat* (1883), it is interesting that, of the two works, they chose the one which was

fig.14 *The gallery at Sidney and Jenny Brown's Villa Langmatt,*
built in 1906 by Karl Moser (photo c. 1914);
on the rear wall, Franz von Stuck's Susanna.

fig.15 *The gallery at Villa Langmatt. On the wall are paintings*
by Van Gogh, Gauguin, Cézanne, Pissarro and Sisley.

fig.16 *Paul Cézanne, Still-Life with Peaches
(Pêches et carafe sur nappe), c. 1900.
Stiftung Langmatt, Sidney and Jenny Brown, Baden.*

fig.17 *Alfred Sisley, The Church at Moret
(L'Eglise de Moret), 1893. Stiftung Langmatt,
Sidney and Jenny Brown, Baden.*

fig.18 *Félix Vallotton, Portrait of Hedy Hahnloser-Bühler, 1908.
Former Hahnloser Collection, Winterthur.*

the most visually appealing. Although the Browns owned some works by Carl Montag, they mostly eschewed works by Swiss Modernists such as Hodler, Amiet, Giacometti and Vallotton, unlike other contemporary collectors.[25] In fact, they exchanged Vallotton's *Bain Turc* with Viau for Sisley's *Eglise de Moret* of 1893 [fig.17].[26] After 1919 the Browns turned their attention to French 18th-century art, financing this shift in taste through the sale of some Impressionist works. They returned enthusiastically to collecting 19th-century art after 1930.

Hedy and Arthur Hahnloser-Bühler's collection in Winterthur is very different from that of the Browns. They were attracted less to classic Impressionism than to Post-Impressionism, the Nabis and the Fauves, as well as to modern Swiss masters. The collection began with the purchase of the landscape by Hodler in 1907, followed soon after by works by Giovanni Giacometti, Cuno Amiet and Carl Montag. Montag introduced the Hahnloser-Bühlers to various artists and dealers, but their collection mostly reflects the taste of their life-long friend, the artist Félix Vallotton [fig.18]. The Hahnlosers' energetic support of Vallotton began in 1908 with their purchase of his *Baigneuses* painted the previous year; eventually they assembled a large collection of his work that embraced the full spectrum of his production, dating from 1882 until his death in 1925. Through Vallotton they came to know the Nabis, in particular Bonnard, Vuillard and Ker-Xavier Roussel [fig.19], whose works feature in their collection, as do those of Henri Matisse, Albert Marquet, Jean Puy, Odilon Redon and Aristide Maillol. The Hahnlosers were exceptional in being personally involved with the artists whose works they collected; in their letters, the artists express intense interest in the growth of their friends' collection at the Villa Flora, and also discuss more intimate worries concerning health or family problems.

The Hahnlosers' involvement with their chosen artists extended beyond their own collection: they actively encouraged friends and family to share their enthusiasm, and Hedy Hahnloser became an art critic, the author of many articles, books and catalogues which supported 'her' artists.[27] The Hahnlosers also lent generously to exhibitions. As early as 1913 their works were featured in the exhibition Französische Bilder aus der Schweiz, organised by Carl Montag in Stuttgart. The extent of their commitment to this art can be seen in their engagement in the public sector, their crucial roles in the reorientation of the Winterthur Kunstverein and the planning, design and construction of the new museum building completed in 1916.

It is curious that Pierre Courthion, in his 1929 account of Swiss collections of French art, chose to include a strongly dismissive passage on Félix Vallotton:

> Vallotton, the painter of a portrait of Mme Hahnloser, is always dry and exact. There are magnificent passages, but on the other hand one finds nothing which pleases, nothing distinct or exceptional [*ajouté*]. There is a total lack of imagination and fantasy with Vallotton. It is the impoverished painting of one who is too great an observer: much science and little art.[28]

One can hardly imagine that these words could be received as anything but an affront by the Hahnlosers, who gave prominence to Vallotton's works in their collection and had so often received him at the Villa Flora as their intimate friend. Vallotton moved from Lausanne to Paris in 1882 to study at the Académie Julian. By the early 1890s he had established a reputation as a woodblock printer and had become acquainted with the Nabis, that group of second-generation Symbolist artists which included Maurice Denis, Edouard Vuillard, Pierre Bonnard, Paul Sérusier and Ker-Xavier Roussel. Vallotton introduced the Hahnlosers to Bonnard and Henri Manguin, and Hedy Hahnloser acknowledged this aspect of Vallotton's relationship with them:

fig.19 *Hedy and Arthur Hahnloser in the garden of Villa Flora, Winterthur.
Standing, left to right: Ker-Xavier Roussel, Richard Bühler,
Jeanne Manguin, Arthur Hahnloser;
foreground seated: Hedy Hahnloser, Henri Manguin.*

fig.20 *Giovanni Giacometti, Portrait of Richard Bühler sailing, Silsersee, 1911. Private Collection.*

fig.21 *Cover of auction catalogue Sammlung Richard Kisling, 18 November 1929, Zunfthaus zur Meise, Zurich. Galerie G. & L. Bollag.*

fig.22 *Gertrud Dübi-Müller's small drawing-room with the portrait by Van Gogh which she bought in 1908, aged 19.*

With uncommon generosity Vallotton inspired us to purchase pictures by his colleagues, and with great enthusiasm helped with the selection of the first Bonnard, Vuillard and Roussel. Only then did we see how unjustifiably the critics had set his work up in opposition to that of his circle of friends.[29]

Hedy Hahnloser's enthusiasm for the Swiss artist (who obtained French citizenship in 1900) is evident, too, in the monograph she wrote in 1936. Courthion, though his subject was the greatness of the private collections in Switzerland, was apparently oblivious to Vallotton's special place in the Hahnloser-Bühler collection, and had little insight into the Hahnlosers' personalities, especially the importance of their direct relationship with the artist.

In her catalogue introduction to the 1940 Lucerne exhibition of her own collection, Hedy Hahnloser also points to the decisive role of Giovanni Giacometti [fig.20]:

> The renewal of our [Swiss] art came, like that in most countries, from Paris. Giovanni Giacometti was one of the first to demonstrate this as he picked up the secrets of the great Impressionists. It was he in Switzerland who spoke with great enthusiasm of Cézanne, prophetically predicting the light that would emanate from that star. Unfortunately it was only later that we had the courage to live up to this message.[30]

Josef Müller was also an energetic advocate of Swiss modern art, collecting Hodler and Amiet, and later Karl Walser, Alexandre Blanchet and Hans Berger. Müller's

enthusiasm for collecting was fired by contact with two older collections, those of Oskar Miller and Richard Kisling. Müller knew the Miller family well, having attended school with Oskar Miller's son. Oskar Miller's remarkable collection of modern Swiss art housed at Biberist stimulated Müller's interest and, through Miller, Josef Müller came to know Giovanni Giacometti and his sons Alberto and Diego. Miller's advocacy of modern art was proclaimed in an article published in 1909 in which he enthusiastically describes his response to the work of Hodler, Amiet, Giacometti, Auberjonois and Trachsel:

> ... The richness of the unity of red and green was my only object, my whole soul.... Colour is its own mother; colour is also the mother of visible line; in the end colour is also the mother of visible planes and spaces. All visual arts share one aspect: the eye that finds its happiness in pure colour.[31]

Müller made his first purchase in 1907: Cuno Amiet's *Mädchen mit Blume* (1907). The collection of Richard Kisling, which Müller had seen in Zurich, also influenced him [fig.21];[32] it was Kisling who introduced the young collector to Hodler in 1909. In August 1909 Müller bought *Die Empfindung* from an exhibition in Interlaken, a picture he had already admired in 1907. He bought works from the early exhibitions of Swiss modern artists and of French painters. The exhibition of French Masters in the Künstlerhaus in Zurich in July 1908 is recorded in Müller's sketchbook. He purchased *L'Asile* later that year. His sister Gertrud Müller, a pupil of Amiet, was an equally active collector and enthusiast for modern art [fig.22]. Her first purchase, made in April 1908 from the O. Miethke art gallery in Vienna via an intermediary, was Van Gogh's *Portrait of Trabuc, an Attendant of St Paul's Hospital, St Rémy* [cat.69]. In 1911 Josef added works by Cézanne. On the advice of the dealer Ambroise Vollard, he acquired the monumental late *Portrait de Vallier* [fig.23]. Cézanne's *Garçon accoudé à la blouse bleue*, from the famous Meyer-Fierz collection in Zurich, followed in 1919 via the Galerie Tanner, Zurich.[33] Müller was open to the counsel of various advisers, including Felix Fénéon, director of Galerie Bernheim-Jeune in Paris, and Cuno Amiet, who encouraged the purchase of Renoir's *Bulgarian Blouse* in 1914. Significantly, that same year works by Kandinsky and Picasso entered Müller's collection. Works by Degas and Matisse (*Notre-Dame de Paris*) followed in 1919 via Galerie Paul Vallotton. In 1923 Müller visited Africa, and the impact of his travels prompted him to assemble one of the most extensive collections of the art of that continent in Europe. By the 1930s Müller had also acquired seven Braques, three Juan Gris, some

ten important works by Léger, ten by Miró dating from 1926–7, some thirty works by Rouault and further works by Renoir. Müller was undoubtedly one of the great collectors of this century, not only because of the high quality of each purchase but because of the breadth of his collection. Indeed, it would be a distortion to limit Müller's collecting activity to the realm of French Impressionism. His aesthetic curiosity and appreciation of art was constrained neither by national chauvinism, nor by trends and developments in Western European art, but reached out to embrace non-European art with a daring and brilliance which presages later understanding of the impact of 'primitive' art on the tradition of Modernism. Photographs of his homes offer glimpses of works by Cézanne, Renoir [fig.25], Amiet, Hodler, Bonnard, Léger, Matisse, Miro, Derain and Picasso, as well as Benin, Dogon and Greek objects. Impressionism represents only one phase in a much more extensive journey in collecting.

Rudolf Staechelin first collected painters from French-speaking Switzerland: Emile Bressler, Gustave François, Edouard Vallet, Maurice Barraud and Benjamin Vautier [fig.24]. He also acquired a number of masterly works by Hodler, almost all from the artist's late, 'classic' period. This predilection for the mature period of an artist's œuvre became a characteristic of Staechelin's collection, which also featured Renoir's late monumental works, classical Cézanne compositions and paintings from Pissarro's plein-air period.

Fauve pictures by Van Dongen, Vlaminck and Derain were also represented in the collection, purchased at the Ludwig Schames Kunstsalon or at M. Goldschmidt & Cie in Frankfurt.

Around 1917 the classic modern French artists – Pissarro, Cézanne, Gauguin, Van Gogh – came to dominate Staechelin's collection. Camille Pissarro was represented, for instance, with seven works. As early as 1912 Staechelin had purchased a work by him from an exhibition of French art at the Basel Kunsthalle, further evidence of the importance of early temporary exhibitions for the emerging collectors.[34] Particularly during World War I, Staechelin depended on the major dealers in modern French art in Switzerland: Moos in Geneva, Vallotton in Lausanne, Tanner and Bollag in Zurich and Thannhauser in Lucerne, although he did acquire Van Gogh's *Tête de femme* direct from Thannhauser in Munich. Around Christmas 1917, that artist's monumental *Berceuse*, now in the Walter Annenberg collection, followed from Tanner. Early in 1918 Staechelin purchased from Vallotton in Lausanne Van Gogh's *Daubigny's Garden with a Black Cat* [cat.70], which he had seen in the Exposition de Peinture Française at the Kunsthalle Basel early in 1917.

Records from 1919 reveal the determination and concentration with which the collection was formed. Within just a few years Staechelin had spent over 700,000 Swiss francs on works by Daumier, Courbet, Fantin-Latour, Manet, Sisley, Renoir, Pissarro, Monet, Gauguin, Van Gogh, Cézanne, Picasso and also Hodler.

fig.23 *A room in Josef Müller's home, Schanzmühle; wall showing works by Cézanne, including the Portrait of the Gardener Vallier (Portrait de Vallier, bought 1911).*

fig.24 *Rudolf Staechelin with his son Peter, Christmas 1926.*

fig.25 *Josef Müller in his living room with a wall of works by Renoir.*

Individual purchases reveal the collector's daring. In Gauguin's *NAFEA Faa-ipoipo* [cat.26], Staechelin chose a challenging figural work from the artist's Tahitian period. This picture, purchased from Galerie Moos in 1917, had been part of the Meyer-Fierz collection in Zurich.[35] The sequence of purchases reveals the breadth, too, of Staechelin's interest. For instance, within just a few days of acquiring *NAFEA*, Picasso's *Les Deux Frères* entered the collection. Staechelin's choice of works by Picasso – *Les Deux Frères* (1906), *Arlequin au loup* (1918), *Arlequin assis* (1923) – follows the artist's career chronologically without, however, including the central and crucial chapter of Cubism. Staechelin clearly preferred works by Picasso from the Rose and Blue periods or from his 'classicising' phase that harmonised with his collection of French 19th-century art.[36]

The pace of Staechelin's collecting slackened significantly in the 1920s, although major purchases include Picasso's *Arlequin assis* from the Galerie Rosenberg in 1924 and Matisse's *Madame Matisse au châle de Manille* purchased from Siegfried Rosengart in 1943. Staechelin remained an active champion of modern French art as a member of the board of the Kunstmuseum in Basel. He was a generous supporter of exhibitions in Basel, lending a significant portion of his collection to the Kunsthalle in 1920.[37] He also contributed to the monographic shows which the curator Wilhelm Barth staged at the Kunsthalle: a Cézanne exhibition in 1921, Van Gogh in 1924, Gauguin in 1929, Matisse in 1931. This tradition of generosity continues today in the form of loans from the Rudolf Staechelin Family Foundation to the Basel Kunstmuseum and other major institutions. Staechelin's own subsequent collecting activity changed in focus, however, and was devoted increasingly to East Asian art; that collection was shown in an exhibition at the Kunsthalle in 1922. There is a parallel between Staechelin's interest in Asian art and Josef Müller's avid collecting of non-Western art, a parallel hinting at a broader tendency in the history of taste and collecting in these decades, a reflection perhaps of a philosophical orientation which Carl Einstein described as a '*Projekt einer Kunstgeschichte der Welt*'.[38]

IMPRESSIONISM, A RADICAL CHOICE: ISSUES OF NATIONALISM AND INTERNATIONALISM

The daring quality of these pioneer collectors is perhaps difficult to understand today. Impressionism was still a controversial style, a 'new' taste which supplanted the established aesthetic hierarchy in which German art – the Munich School in particular – was placed at the apogee. The dramatic change is evident,

fig.26 *Pierre-Auguste Renoir, After the Bath (Après le bain), 1912. Kunstmuseum Winterthur.*

for instance, in photographs of Jenny and Sidney Brown's Villa Langmatt in Baden, in which German paintings are gradually substituted by Impressionist pictures. The Browns, whose collection had included large-scale compositions by Franz von Stuck, Gotthardt Kühl and Ludwig Herevich, were reticent to reveal their newer purchases to their Baden neighbours and for some time timidly reserved their Impressionist pictures for their private quarters. Hedy Hahnloser-Bühler, whose own aesthetic orientation had also initially been directed towards Munich where she had studied painting and design, chided Carl Montag in 1905 for having abandoned his German cultural identity to 'kneel before the superficial refinements of the French'.[39]

This reorientation in taste did not go unchallenged. Admittedly, a work by Pissarro was acquired by the Basel Kunstmuseum in 1912,[40] and, after 1912, the forward-looking board of the Kunstverein in Winterthur had steered the Kunstmuseum's acquisitions towards French modern art by purchasing a landscape by Marquet in 1915. However, as late as 1917, the proposed acquisition of a seated nude, Renoir's *Après le bain* [fig.26], by the Kunstmuseum Winterthur was greeted with vehement disapproval at a public meeting of the Kunstverein.[41] That Renoir was still seen, even at this date, as an example of the avant-garde, is confirmed by the enthusiasm of the radical critic and champion of modern art Meier-Graefe for the artist's paintings of bathers of the mid-1880s. Writing in 1928, Meier-Graefe especially praised Renoir's late work as a manifestation of the great tradition of French painting: 'Renoir was the first to see through the dubious social side of modern art, the "splendid isolation" of individualism, and to release himself (so far as it is possible in our time) from the "I" and to move toward universality.'[42]

The new museum at Winterthur, designed by Rittmeyer and completed in 1916 [fig.27], still had to rely on loans from the major local collections in order to represent modern French art to the public. It was thus that the Franzosensaal was inaugurated, dependent upon a changing display of loans illustrating the development of French art from Daumier and Delacroix to Picasso and Matisse [fig.28]. The move from private home to public gallery for the new art was reinforced three years later by Hans Schuler's donation of his collection to the Kunsthaus in Zurich.[43]

An important component in the controversy surrounding the shift in taste from German to French, from Böcklin to Cézanne, was the argument that the new French art demanded narrative and poetic meaning to be abandoned in favour of neutral compositions of figural, landscape and still-life subjects. In the mainstream critical evaluation of the 1880s and '90s, Böcklin was celebrated as the heroic embodiment of the German imagination and spirit. Meier-Graefe's formalist methods and his insistence on a single painterly tradition culminating in French Impressionism (effectively excluding Böcklin from consideration) were interpreted as radical attacks on both art and nation. Meier-Graefe's critics frequently combined aesthetic judgements with cultural chauvinism in their attacks. In his 1901 article entitled 'Monet und Böcklin', Karl Scheffler wrote: 'With the Impressionists everything is dead, only light lives; with Böcklin the smallest flower lives, every element has its own living entity and everything harmoniously works together.'[44] For Fritz Ostini, Böcklin was simply 'urdeutsch'.[45] The aesthetic and the political came together in Switzerland when the confrontation of French Impressionist and German Idealist painting was used by chauvinistic commentators in arguments often charged with undisguised racism (linked, of course, to attacks in Germany on Meier-Graefe, Paul and Bruno Cassirer and Max Liebermann). For neutral Switzerland, despite its proud tradition of independence and democracy, and because of its unique linguistic and cultural amalgam, there was an uncomfortable and inevitable tendency toward cultural definition via France or Germany, a dilemma which underlines this controversy. In Switzerland the choice between German and French art, between Böcklin and the Impressionists, involved a reorientation in personal and national self-definition. One cannot overestimate the importance of Swiss artists such as Hodler and Amiet who offered an international outlook as an alternative to nationalistic chauvinism.[46] The potential for chauvinistic controversy is readily apparent, for instance, in an exchange which appeared in the journal *Wissen und Leben* concerning the 1908 Impressionist exhibition in Zurich. The vituperative debate began with the comments of the reactionary architect Alexander von Senger whose purported subject is the regretted absence in Impressionist art of the 'poetry' for which Böcklin was famed. He deplored the disturbing passivity of the Impressionists' supposed unfiltered copying of nature's chaotic impulses. Von Senger's real subject soon becomes apparent: a racially motivated condemnation of Impressionism as the bankrupt non-art of an impure culture:

> French painting no longer exists; in its place a totally new painting with new concepts has come to exist; it suffices to compare traditional French painting with Impressionist painting – a true Negro or Mongolian art, to make the spiritual regression clear … In Germany we already see a huge troop of enthusiastic Impressionists, of course under oriental leadership.[47]

The Zurich collector Hans Schuler made a spirited response to this undisguised racist polemic. Dismissing the pseudo-scientific pretensions of Von Senger's anthropological racism, Schuler focused his attention on the fragments of aesthetic and art-historical argumentation in Von Senger's article. In direct opposition to Von Senger, and perhaps drawing on recent publications on Impressionism by Harry Graf Kessler or Meier-Graefe, Schuler posits Impressionism as part of an organic and logical historical development. For Schuler the question of whether the painting is elaborated before the motif or in the studio, whether this process is immediate or laboured over a long period of time, are not grounds for judging artistic merit. The impact of Meier-Graefe's formalist criticism seems clear: extra-painterly qualities – 'Poetry based on a philosophical view of life'– so crucial for Von Senger, are for Schuler less important than technique and style which directly express artistic personality in the simplest and the most elaborate compositions.[48] E. Bovet, the publisher of *Wissen und Leben*, directly challenged Von Senger's Pan-Germanic politics with a celebration of independent Swiss culture: 'Instead of race we propose the nation; instead of hatred, civilisation; instead of blind nature, conscience; it is, in the physical universe, mankind's glorious creation; in the night of slaveries, it is the path that mounts towards light and liberty.'[49]

fig.27 *Kunstmuseum Winterthur, designed by Robert Rittmeyer; completed 1916, opened 1917.*

fig.28 *The 'Franzosensaal' (French Room) in the new Kunstmuseum, Winterthur, with works from the collection of the Kunstverein and long-term loans from private collections. The left wall shows paintings by Vallotton; on the right, the works include those by Odilon Redon and Renoir.*

Three years later, in a text entitled 'Meier-Graefe und Van Gogh', the Swiss artist Albert Welti expressed his undisguised resentment of what he perceived to be the rejection of his master, Böcklin, in favour of the French Impressionists. His arguments range from a straightforward dismissal of Van Gogh's '*formlose and farbenkrasse Nudeleien*' to a lamentation of the disintegration of cultural life in Germany:

> Unfortunately since the time of Schiller and Goethe, a large part of the German nation has lost its vision. Yet it was not only with blindness, but also without character, the way in which the educated Germans were so quickly converted from Böcklin's art to that of some of the French Impressionists. Those which made the biggest impression on them were those that entirely lacked an honest naturalism, and who attempted to simulate free invention and fantasy with any sort of dancing daubs of the brush.

Welti concludes with character assassinations of Meier-Graefe and other supporters of Impressionism: 'Meier-Graefe. Scholar with a dealer's heart…. It is no longer about scholarship, but rather about sensationalism and financial interests.'[50]

These ideological battles were (as they often are today) played out in the cultural-political arena and focused on state sponsorship and funding of the arts. Conservatives complained about the 'Hodlerisation' of the Swiss submissions to international exhibitions as well as the hegemony of that style or group in national settings, for example exhibitions and official commissions. In a pamphlet of 1911, Dr Johannes Winkler frets about this misrepresentation of Swiss art. He suspects the Hodler group of importing foreign influences:

> Another artistic manifestation, Impressionism, has its typical Swiss representative in Cuno Amiet. The Impressionists placed colouristic effects over the meaning of the subject, indeed over the real truth. Cuno Amiet is the agent of French Impressionism imported ready-made into Switzerland, a style which has long since become international.[51]

In late 1913 and early 1914 the Swiss Parliament wrestled with the issues of public subsidies for the arts and the proper representation of Swiss art abroad, and their debates in turn unleashed heated discussions in the press. Voices from abroad were sometimes interjected, and were not always welcome. One year earlier, articles and brochures had debated the quality and the prominence given to Hodler and the avant-garde in the Swiss entry to the International Exhibition at the Glaspalast in Munich.[52] In spring 1914 a group of Swiss

artists, architects and writers living in Munich added their voices to the debate in the form of an open letter. It is ironic that their defence of Hodler depended partially on differentiating him from the 'aesthetic decadence' identified with urban culture and from foreign art such as Cubism and Futurism.[53]

The continuing debate on the national significance of art was exceedingly confusing. In 1913, Impressionism, once revolutionary, was described as a thoroughly acceptable historical phenomenon, even relatively conservative (at least in comparison with Cubism or Futurism), and invoked to defend Hodler from attack:

> In observing the Impressionist exhibition as a whole, one would be hard pressed to understand how many of them were considered revolutionary or even deranged and how their exhibitions could be seen as cabinets of horror. For us today many of their pictures are no longer upsetting, indeed we see them almost as Old Master works, as something historical. This should give second thoughts to those who would fight and laugh at modern painting such as Hodler's.[54]

Within a short period of time, and depending on the author's cultural-political perspective, Hodler is used to represent either a dreaded internationalism or the paradigm of Swiss art, of a '*Schweizerisch-nationale Einheits Kultur*'.[55] The politicisation of Impressionism intensified during World War I when both the French and the German governments attempted to use culture in the service of propaganda. Harry Graf Kessler was assigned to the German Embassy in Bern with the task of promoting German art in exhibitions in Switzerland. The success with which Carl Montag launched a variety of exhibition projects featuring French painting resulted in the award of the Commandeur de Légion d'Honneur.[56] In the end, despite the efforts of factions in the government and military to tilt sentiment towards Germany, Switzerland maintained its neutrality, and its cultural-political orientation was inclined decidedly in favour of France.

The debates on foreign influence and the purity of Swiss culture apparently outlived the war. In 1919, for instance, Hedy Hahnloser-Bühler responded with outrage to statements published by the artist Ernst Würtenberger on the undue influence of French art and the impact of Paris-based galleries in Switzerland. Hahnloser questions whether the market for traditional Swiss artists is really so precarious, given the sustained high prices paid for works by Böcklin and Welti. She emphatically supported Swiss artists ranging from Vallotton to Hodler and Würtenberger. This seems ironic if one recalls that it is Würtenberger's portrait of the new members of the Kunstverein in Winterthur [fig.1] which documents the energy and vision of that group of dynamic young collectors. Hahnloser, proud of her personal involvement with the artists she supported, reacted with sensitivity to Würtenberger's insinuation that the Winterthur collections were in the pocket of the Parisian galleries – 'Filiale Bernheim-Jeune in Winterthur' – and argues, following Meier-Graefe, that her interest in French art was inevitable, as it is manifestly *the* great modern expression of *the* great tradition of painting.[57]

The excitement and vigour with which the Swiss collected French modern art from the turn of the century to the end of World War I parallels the energy that they brought to their work as physicians, engineers, industrialists and entrepreneurs. Their need for a new and modern art form fits their positive, progressive vision of the world. The journal *Wissen und Leben*, published by an organisation of the same name founded in 1907, is a telling example of this idealistic point of view. Bringing together leaders from every possible field to explore the great themes and problems of humanity on the threshold of a new age, the group hoped to establish a dialogue which could help inform and mould the individual to face the challenges of the future. The members of this organisation, the leaders of Switzerland, the collectors of French modern art, shared a progressive and idealistic faith in the present and future. The abrupt dissolution of this optimism in the wake of the Great War is eloquently expressed in Georg Reinhart's preface to the catalogue of his collection that he published privately in 1922:

> In the end the World War and the ensuing economic chaos, whose end we still cannot perceive, put a damper on the naïve joy in collecting; a feeling of insecurity about what the coming years would bring in the context of economics, politics and culture, became an obstacle.[58]

Collecting would, of course, continue despite the political and economic tension that rent Switzerland with nationwide strikes in 1919, through economic upswings and downturns, even through another world war and certainly through the subsequent prosperous decades. But the stage had been irrevocably altered, and the Impressionist and Post-Impressionist picture had become the most sought-after prize in the international arena.   [DK]

After the war [1914–18], a new type of purchaser made its presence felt: the industrialist. One could well say that there were probably no great names in Swiss industry that were not also known as collectors of repute: Sulzer, Dubied, Dübi, Abegg, Stoll, Rom, Stierlin, Firmenich, Junod, Von Hirsch, Rupf, Rosengart, Staehlin [sic], Sydney Brown are names which were no longer solely associated with locomotives, sewing machines, watches, pharmaceuticals, chocolate, shoes, perfumes, commercial banking or other branches of business and industry; they were also associated with pictures by Courbet, Corot, Daumier, Delacroix, Manet, Cézanne, Renoir, Gauguin, Van Gogh, Rouault, Picasso and Klee....[59]

Cabanne's description of the pattern of private collecting in Switzerland immediately after the end of World War I summarises succinctly the results of a period of intense activity by her collectors both prior to and during the four years of international conflict. The story of the succeeding decade was, in many instances, to be one of consolidation. The Hahnlosers, the Sulzers, the Mettlers and the Bühlers, for example, continued to strengthen their collections, buying increasingly through the recently established Swiss galleries as much as through the artist-advisers and Parisian dealers with whom they had dealt before 1914.[60] However, some of the pioneer collections came to an abrupt halt through the death of their initiators: Hans Schuler died in 1920, bequeathing his collection to the Kunsthaus Zurich;[61] Fritz Meyer-Fierz had died in 1917 and his collection was finally dispersed in a sale nine years later at Muller & Cie, Amsterdam.[62] Others either temporarily or more permanently diversified their collections by moving into new areas of art. The Browns at Baden put almost all their efforts during this decade into buying 18th-century French painting and decorative arts, and Josef Müller, following a formative trip to Africa, began collecting the art of that continent in 1923.[63] Willy Russ-Suchard pursued his enthusiasm for Hodler to the extent that, in order to increase his holdings of the artist's work, he divested himself between 1922 and 1924 of major works by Courbet, Daumier, Renoir, Vuillard and Van Gogh and a Picasso.[64]

However, new and important collections were also created immediately after the end of hostilities. Some concentrated more exclusively on Impressionism and Post-Impressionism, while others embarked on more ambitious journeys, acquiring works across the history of art with the intention of giving the modern

fig.29 *Georg Reinhart.*

fig.30 *Oskar Reinhart.*

fig.31 *Prints and Drawings Room in the new Kunstmuseum, Winterthur (designed by Robert Rittmeyer). Oskar Reinhart held the position of 'custodian'.*

movements a historical context. Dr Auguste Widmer, proprietor of a clinic at Valmont, limited his collecting to the modern French artists. Between 1917 and 1928, he bought, primarily through the Galerie Paul Vallotton in Lausanne, still-lifes by Manguin and Cézanne; landscapes by Jongkind, Renoir, Bonnard and Marquet; several works by Félix Vallotton and two works by Degas: *Portrait d'homme* and *Femme s'essuyant*. On his death the entire collection was bequeathed to the Musée Cantonal, Lausanne.[65]

Perhaps the most notable collection to be amassed in the 1920s was that of Oskar Reinhart. Oskar Reinhart was born into a family in which art and music were much appreciated. His father, Theodor Reinhart, the owner of the international trading company Volkart, had started collecting works by contemporary Swiss and German artists in the 1880s, including Karl Hofer and the Lucerne landscape painter Zünd. He was also one of the first in Switzerland to collect Hodler, persuading the Winterthur Kunstverein to purchase one of his works for the Kunstmuseum in 1899. This enthusiasm for collecting was passed down to at least two of his four sons, Georg and Oskar.[66] The elder, Georg [fig.29], had staked out his interest in the new French taste which had recently 'invaded' Winterthur when he purchased from Durand-Ruel in the autumn of 1911 a *Baigneuse* by Renoir[67] and a work by Marquet. Over the following twelve months he expanded the collection in this field by buying works by Cézanne (*Marronnier du Jas de Bouffan*), Gauguin, Degas and Renoir.[68] He then proceeded to surround these works with their immediate artistic predecessors, represented, as argued by Meier-Graefe, by Corot, Delacroix, Daumier and Goya.[69] The fruits of his collection were published in a private catalogue which appeared in 1922.[70]

Oskar Reinhart [fig.30] was to reflect his elder brother's desire to provide a context for the French Impressionists and Post-Impressionists, but his ambitions were far greater. Although he only started collecting in earnest in 1919, he had, while representing the company abroad before 1914, spent time studying art, especially graphic art.[71] This led him not only to amass an important collection of prints (including works by the British etcher Muirhead Bone) but also earned him the position of 'custodian' of the Print Room at the Kunstmuseum Winterthur [fig.31], where he both organised exhibitions, often with works drawn from his own collection, and edited the journal, *Das graphische Kabinett*. From 1919, and particularly between 1924 and 1936, he bought works by Old Masters, French 19th-century artists, from David, Delacroix and Ingres to Daumier, Courbet, the Impressionists, Gauguin, Van Gogh and Toulouse-Lautrec [fig.32], and followed his father's taste by collecting contemporary Swiss artists. In 1924 he retired from the family business and moved into his new home, Am Römerholz, designed between 1913 and 1915 by the Geneva architect Maurice Turrettini, onto which in the same year he built a picture gallery [fig.33]. The richness of his holdings was first made public in an exhibition held in Basel in 1932, and in 1951 the collection of Swiss, German and Austrian art was given as a foundation to Winterthur. Seven years later, the rest of the

fig.32 *Oskar Reinhart in 1955.*
On the wall hangs Toulouse-Lautrec's La Clownesse.

fig.33 *House and garden, Am Römerholz,*
Winterthur (architect: Maurice Turrettini, 1913–5),
the home of Oskar Reinhart after 1924.

fig.34 *Paul Vallotton (right), with his brother Félix, the painter,*
Champéry, 1921.

collection was given to the State, together with Am Römerholz. Reinhart died in 1965.[72]

In 1928, Oskar Reinhart walked into an art gallery in Munich. It was owned by Fritz Nathan, and the visitor bought not a French Impressionist painting, but a work by Waldmüller, *Salzburg bei Ischl*.[73] Reinhart relied heavily on Fritz Nathan and other dealers for the spectacular accumulation of his collection during the 1920s and 1930s. The Hahnlosers and the Bühlers also had recourse to Galerie Paul Vallotton in Lausanne, and other major collectors resorted to a group of dealers in Zurich, including Neupert, Tanner and Wolfensberger. This suggests that the source of works for purchase during the 1920s was shifting from the individual intermediary and adviser, for example Carl Montag and Félix Vallotton, and the galleries in Paris, Munich and Berlin, to the dealer and home-based galleries in Switzerland. Fuelled by the remarkable growth in private collecting and the temporary exhibitions mounted by the Kunstverein, the first commercial galleries to specialise in French modern painting emerged in Zurich shortly after 1910. These tended to be the creations of prominent Parisian and Berlin dealers who wished to establish a presence within a fast developing market. Thus Bernheim-Jeune of Paris was represented in Zurich from April 1913 by Gustav Tanner, and in August of the same year the gallery gained access to Suisse Romande by opening the Galerie Paul Vallotton in Lausanne [fig.34]. Ambroise Vollard, however, had beaten Bernheim-Jeune to Zurich through an informal relationship, brokered by Carl Montag, with the print publisher and dealer, J.E. Wolfensberger. In October 1911, Wolfensberger

opened a new gallery, the Kunstsalon Wolfsberg, in Bederstrasse, in the suburbs of Zurich. The following March, Wolfensberger held a major exhibition of work by Paul Gauguin, the stock seemingly supplied by Ambroise Vollard [fig.35]. This exhibition was visited by Michael Sadler, the British civil servant and future Vice-Chancellor of the University of Leeds. On a brief vacation in Gersau on the Vierwaldstättersee, he had spotted an announcement of the exhibition in a Lucerne newspaper:

> The Gauguin exhibition turned out to be in a new Gallery [sic], in a suburb of Zurich, recently opened by Wolfsberg [sic], the firm of colour-printers. The top gallery is one of the pleasantest I have ever seen: white paint: sacking walls: grey linoleum floor with Afghan red rugs and pale wicker chairs. The Gauguins were all (wisely) hung together in a separate gallery – the nine oils in one room, and about ten lithographs in another. 'Joseph and Potiphar's Wife' (about the size of 'L'Esprit Veille') is by far the finest of the nine in colour. The 'reverie' is the most touching and (I thought) the greatest of the lot. The early Pisaroish [sic] 'Enfants dans la forêt' is of small account. The 'Ronde des bretonnes' is the transition from Pisarro [sic] to the stage at which he painted 'La Lutte' which was at Nevill's. There was one picture 'Les Bœufs' of the Brittany period – very singular and archaistic – two long bullocks standing worshipping before a shrine – Christmas Eve, snow on the cottage roofs and a stormy sunset behind. The picture is purple and white.[74]

Wolfensberger followed this exhibition with one in the summer entitled Gemälde französischer Meister, consisting of some seventy works, including paintings by Monet, Cézanne, Pissarro, Sisley and Renoir. Wolfensberger again had recourse to Carl Montag as his intermediary with Vollard. Wolfensberger's justification of a summer exhibition was expressed by Montag in a letter to Vollard: '… you certainly know that during these months a large number of foreigners from all different countries come to Switzerland, whereas in Paris you will have a dead season'.[75] Shortly after this exhibition, Montag defected to the gallery run by Gustav Tanner where he was to oversee, among other exhibitions, the first retrospective devoted to Camille Pissarro, held in Switzerland in 1913. The reference to the 'summer season' for foreigners in Switzerland in Montag's letter may also explain the reason for the Munich dealer Thannhauser using Siegfried Rosengart as his representative in Lucerne in 1919 [fig.36]. It was also cited by Fritz Nathan as the reason for his establishment in 1926

fig.35 *Ambroise Vollard, art dealer and publisher, c.1930.*

of a presence during the summer months in Lucerne through the dealer Helbing.[76]

Fritz Nathan was to play a crucial role in the shaping of several major Swiss collections made after c.1930, most notably, Oskar Reinhart, E.G. Bührle, Baron Heinrich Thyssen-Bornemisza (whom he first visited in the summer of 1948)[77] and Jacques Koerfer (from 1951). Born in Munich into a family with a long association with the art trade, Fritz Nathan initially trained as a doctor before joining the gallery run by his elder brother Otto in 1922. In 1926 he inaugurated the 'summer season' of temporary exhibitions in Lucerne. Two years later he met Oskar Reinhart. In 1936 Nathan emigrated from Munich to St Gallen. Two years after that he met the Zurich industrialist and owner of the Oerlikon Works, E.G. Bührle, through the sale of a Van Gogh still-life.[78] During World War II, Nathan continued his activities in Switzerland, but, according to his memoirs, refused to participate in any of the auctions held by Fischer in Lucerne of works seized by the Nazis in France and Germany.[79] In 1951, Nathan moved his gallery to Zurich, where he continued to deal until his death in 1972. Nathan's early association with German Romantic and Realist painting, from Waldmüller to Menzel, Leibl, Thoma and Liebermann, had provided him with his initial contact with Oskar Reinhart in 1928. Reinhart's determination to establish a collection in this field led to further purchases from Nathan, for example, Arnold Böcklin's *Paolo and Francesca* (1893). However, Nathan also moved into French 19th- and early 20th-century art, examples of which found their way into Reinhart's collection,

fig.36 *Galerie Thannhauser, Lucerne, c.1920.*

including Daumier's *La Partie de dames* (1860–3) and Manet's *Portrait de Marguerite de Conflans* (1873).

Fritz Nathan's association with the collector Emil Georg Bührle carries the history of taste for Impressionism and Post-Impressionism in Switzerland into the post-World War II era. Born in Pforzheim in 1890, Bührle moved from Magdeburg to Zurich in 1924, when he took over the Oerlikon Machine Tool Works. He remained in Zurich until his death in 1956. He made his initial purchases in the 1930s, cautiously feeling his way into the more modern period of French art by buying works by Corot, Courbet, Daubigny and Pissarro from one of Zurich's most progressive galleries, Aktuaryus.[80] In 1937, however, he ventured to buy Manet, Cézanne and Van Gogh, acquiring through Siegfried Rosengart (Lucerne) Manet's *Rue Mosnier aux drapeaux*,[81] Cézanne's *Mont Ste Victoire*[82] and Van Gogh's *Olive Orchard*.[83] The following year, he purchased a Van Gogh from Nathan. During the subsequent two decades, Nathan regularly supplied Impressionist and Post-Impressionist paintings for Bührle's collection: Monet, *Vétheuil*[84] in 1941; Manet, *Le Suicide*[85] in 1948; Renoir, *Femme au chapeau de plume*[86] in 1950 and *Les Moissonneurs*[87] in 1951; Van Gogh, *Wheatfield with Cypresses*[88] and *The Sower*[89] in 1951; and Gauguin, *Idylle en Tahiti*[90] in 1952. Three years later, Bührle also purchased from Nathan an Old Master painting, Pieter Jansz. Saenredam's *Interior of St Bavo Church, Haarlem*. This work added to a growing number of major Old Master paintings purchased by Bührle after 1945.[91] Of these, the purchase from Nathan was somewhat exceptional, since Bührle was also buying from galleries in London and New York. He followed this more international pattern for a significant number of his Impressionist and Post-Impressionist works, buying in 1953 from Wildenstein New York and Paris, Gauguin's *Nature morte: panier de fruits et couteau*,[92] from Gallery Knoedler and Co. New York, in the same year, Vuillard's *La Visite*,[93] and works by Pissarro, Manet and Toulouse-Lautrec from other American dealers.[94] This extension of Bührle's sources into an international, and indeed transatlantic, dimension underlines a more general trend in the purchase patterns of Swiss collectors especially after 1945 [fig.37]. This is hardly surprising. With the United States established as the fastest growing and wealthiest economy in the Western world, it also inevitably became the leading centre for the art market. To this must be added the establishment in New York of branches of the major international auction houses, notably Sotheby's and Christie's. However, it would be wrong to suggest that Swiss galleries after c.1950 no longer provided important works for collectors of Impressionism and Post-Impres-

fig.37 *Emil Georg Bührle in his gallery.*
From top left, anticlockwise, works by Bonnard, Van Gogh,
Cézanne, Derain, Picasso, Vallotton and Braque.
Behind Bührle stands Degas's Mme Camus au piano.

shaped by his friendship with the young Swiss painter Gustav Schudel, and he acquired 19th- and 20th-century German and Swiss art, including works by Hodler and François and Aimé Barraud. In the field of French 19th- and 20th-century art, he covered the landscape tradition from Corot and Rousseau, Millet, Boudin and Harpignies, to Sisley, Monet, Pissarro and Cézanne. The collection closed with examples by Marquet, Utrillo, Vlaminck and Kisling.[95] Another collector, who started to acquire important Impressionists around 1933, however, bought primarily outside Switzerland in cities to which he travelled on business, notably London, Paris and New York.[96]

A typical Swiss collection was built up by a prominent member of the Swiss business community over the years spanning World War II. Although this collection started with horse paintings, including works by Géricault and Toulouse-Lautrec, it soon paralleled the taste of collectors such as Sydney Brown: Trouillebert and Boudin, Corot, Monet, Sisley, Renoir, Degas and Cézanne were surrounded by fine examples of French furniture and *objets de vertu*.

The political uncertainties in Europe in the 1930s caused Bernhard Mayer to settle in Zurich, Jacques Koerfer to move from Hamburg to Bern, and Baron Heinrich Thyssen-Bornemisza to purchase the Villa Favorita outside Lugano in 1932. After 1945, major Greek collectors, including Niarchos and Goulandris, took up residence in Switzerland.

In his introduction to the catalogue of the exhibition of 1984 celebrating the wealth of Post-Impressionist and modern French painting in Suisse Romande collections, François Daulte correctly referred to the surprise expressed by the Swiss themselves when they were confronted by Impressionist and Post-Impressionist works in Swiss private collections exhibited at the Palais de Beaulieu, Lausanne, in 1964.[97] The very discretion of individual collectors had led to an absence of recognition up to that date of the full extent, both quantitatively and qualitatively, of the works held in their country. That tradition for collecting has continued in the three decades since that epic exhibition.

SWITZERLAND IN A LARGER PICTURE

In June 1911 the great room of the Winterthur Town Hall housed an exhibition entitled Kunstwerke aus Winterthurer Privatbesitz [fig.38]. As well as showing the modern Swiss artists favoured by the Winterthur collectors – for example Hodler, Amiet, Giovanni Giacometti and Carl Montag – the exhibition also displayed 'modern' French paintings, including works by Renoir, Bonnard, Vallotton, Ker-Xavier Roussel,

sionism. In the German-speaking part of Switzerland, the Galerie Beyeler in Basel, established in 1951, and Walter Feilchenfeldt, who established his gallery in Zurich in 1948 (Feilchenfeldt had been Paul Cassirer's right-hand person in Berlin), were major forces in the construction of collections both in Switzerland and elsewhere, while in French-speaking Switzerland galleries founded before 1939 such as the Galerie Paul Vallotton in Lausanne and the Galerie Moos in Geneva continued actively to trade in these areas.

At this time an increasing number of collections were made by foreigners who had come to settle in Switzerland. Some collections made in the late 1930s and 1940s were created by Swiss nationals, and in some cases acquisitions continued to be made primarily from Swiss sources. This was the case of the collection of Professor Dr Arthur Stoll, a native of Basel who, in 1939, settled on Lake Geneva and constructed an extensive collection through Galerie Moos in Geneva, Lucas Lichtenhan and Willy Raeber in Basel, Siegfried Rosengart in Lucerne and Albin Neupert in Zurich. Stoll had started collecting in 1934. His taste was in part

fig.38 *Ausstellung von Kunstwerken aus Winterthurer Privatbesitz (Winterthur Private Collections), 1911, hung in the Town Hall, Winterthur.*

fig.39 *The Grand Art Hall, Bella Vista Castle, Garrett, New Jersey, 1896, showing the mixture of Impressionist and more conventional 19th-century art amassed by Catholina Lambert. On the top gallery to the left hang works by Sisley, while paintings by Renoir and Monet are displayed on the wall behind P.P. Veretshash's massive view of the Kremlin, Moscow.*

Marquet and Manguin. A German critic writing in the *Schwabische Merkur* compared the calm acceptance of these works in Switzerland in 1911 with the reaction which he feared such work might have provoked in contemporary Germany: '... such audacious modernity [that] in Germany it would only have produced aston-ishment and curiosity.'[98] A few years later, the Paris dealer Ambroise Vollard was staying in Winterthur with the Hahnlosers at the Villa Flora. He recorded a Frenchman's view of a foreign-made collection as follows: '... [The Hahnlosers] are amongst the most avid propagandists and proponents of French art in Switzerland. What a Bonnard collection I was able to view there! And the Renoirs! ... quite simply our entire Modern art.'[99]

Such evaluations of the holdings of 'modern' (that is, Impressionist, Post-Impressionist and early modern) art in Switzerland indicate that even at this early date international comparisons could be made. Thus, it is only appropriate to consider the degree to which Swiss collecting *c.*1900–30 conformed to patterns found elsewhere, both in Europe and in the United States.

For those Swiss collectors who, unlike Arthur and Hedy Hahnloser and Josef and Gertrud Müller, did not embark immediately on the acquisition of contempo-rary modern masters, the conversion of taste involved exploration of the more acceptable aspects of non-academic 19th-century art. This process carried Fritz Meyer-Fierz (1847–1917) from collecting Hague School and Barbizon School artists in the 1880s to the ownership of five Van Goghs purchased from the 1908 Van Gogh exhibition;[100] the Browns from the works of such German artists as Franz von Stuck, Julius Exter and Gotthardt Kuhl via Boudin and Trouillebert in 1896 to Cézanne in 1908. This pattern of 'conversion' is not exceptional when seen within an international context.

In England, Michael Sadler 'graduated' as a collector from William Turner of Oxford, via the Hague School (notably Bauer) to Meryon, Fantin-Latour, Puvis de Chavannes, Cézanne and Gauguin by 1910.[101] And in many American collections, there was a similar logical progression from an enthusiasm for Barbizon School and, in some cases, Hague School paintings which were available through New York galleries such as Knoedler, Avery, Schaus and Cottier. These works formed the starting point of many collections, often complemented by contemporary American paintings [fig.39]. Typical of these is that of William H. Fuller of New York, director of the National Wallpaper Company, whose sizeable collection of Barbizon paintings provided the springboard into a major col-lection of Impressionists which, on his death in 1902, included eleven Monets.[102] Harry Havemayer had started with a collection of 19th-century American painting, but in 1880 he bought a work by the Barbizon School artist Diaz; the following year, he bought from Knoedler & Company two further works by Diaz, one Rousseau, one Corot and one Millet, thus creating a historical context for his and his wife Louisine's formi-dable collection of Impressionist works.[103] More sur-prising was the case of Henry Clay Frick, who between *c.*1890 and 1899, when he purchased Rembrandt's *A Young Painter*, had amassed a significant collection of Barbizon works, including paintings by Daubigny, Rousseau and Troyon as well as examples of the Hague School; such works provided a natural setting for the purchase in 1895 of a painting of Argenteuil by Monet.[104]

The geographic concentration of Swiss pioneering collections was not in itself unusual when viewed within an international context. A similar concentration was evident of Paris. More pertinent to the Swiss situation was perhaps the competitive collecting in Moscow between Sergey Shchukin and Ivan Morosov, the former beginning to develop his collection in the early 1890s, the latter around 1906.[105] A similar pattern occurred in Egypt. Here the three most significant collections, of Mahmoud Mahmoud Khalil, Moise Levy de Benzion and, on a more modest level, Youssef Kamel, were all built up between 1918 and 1939 and were located in Cairo.[106] Likewise, Denmark saw a similar cluster of collectors in Copenhagen.[107] This pattern suggests that, where such activity is undertaken in a country with a relatively small but wealthy and culturally aspiring class, there was a tendency for collections to be gathered in a few centres.

From the 1870s, a group of French collectors, including Félix Faure, Victor Chocquet, Henri Rouart, Hoschedé, Comte Doria, Théodore Duret, Emile Zola, Octave Mirbeau, Moreau-Nelaton and Comte Camondo, and, specifically for Cézanne after 1890, Pellerin, had bought Impressionists and Post-Impressionists. In almost all these cases, these collectors were friends of the artists whose work they collected, in some cases commissioning work from them (Chocquet), in others supporting them through articles and reviews as much as through the purchase of their work (Zola, Duret, Octave Mirbeau). In the United States, the taste for Impressionism was also established earlier than in Switzerland. A disreputable bond dealer, Erwin Davies, who was hounded out of San Francisco and ultimately settled in New York, sent the artist Alden Weir to Paris in 1881 specifically to purchase two works by Manet, *Garçon à l'épée* and *Femme au perroquet* (both in The Metropolitan Museum of Art) and a Degas

Dancers.[108] At the Pedastal exhibition held two years later in New York at the National Academy of Design, he lent thirty-seven works, and in April 1886 he was to buy four Monets from Durand-Ruel's exhibition held in that city. More famously, there was the case of Mary Cassatt who not only introduced her friend, Louisine Havemayer, wife of Harry, to Impressionism during her second trip to Paris in 1875, but also encouraged such other early collectors as her brother, Alexander Cassatt of Philadelphia, vice-president of the Pennsylvania Railroad, and Annie Scott, a relation of Louisine Havemayer.[109] Such was the disposable income of many of the early American collectors that they were also able to cross the Atlantic to buy direct from the galleries in Paris. Furthermore, from 1886, Paris dealers established a presence on American soil, with Durand-Ruel opening a gallery in New York in 1886, and Boussod & Valadon opening one two years later. The relatively more established galleries such as Knoedler and Co. and Cottier also concentrated on buying more modern art. By the end of the 1890s, significant collections of Impressionist and Post-Impressionist works had been built up in New York (Havemayer, Fuller), Philadelphia (Alexander Cassatt and the lawyer John S. Johnson), Chicago (Palmer Potter), Boston (Desmond Fitzgerald) and Cleveland (Pope) [fig.40].

If Switzerland was somewhat behind collecting 'modern' art compared to either France or the United States, its collections were nonetheless more focused, and were developed far faster than the somewhat haphazard collections formed elsewhere in Europe. In the United Kingdom, for example, before the creation of the major collections of Samuel Courtauld, Chester Beatty and Alexander Maitland (and William Burrell as far as Impressionist works were concerned), the story of the development of a taste for French 'modern' art was episodic. It ranged from Mr Henry Hill, a tailor from Marine Parade, Brighton, buying five or six Impressionist paintings from Durand-Ruel before the latter closed his London gallery in 1876, to Mr Burke, who in the 1890s bought from Durand-Ruel two Pissarros (1892), two Sisleys (1893), a Degas (*La Pédicure*, 1898) and one Pissarro (1899). There were also those who moved in the circle of Sickert, himself a collector and advocate of the work of Degas in particular, for example the Unwin Fishers, or those who had studied in Paris and hence come into contact with the new art. One such figure was Mrs Ethel Sutro, who shared with the Unwin Fishers the distinction of having been the first owners of Van Goghs in the United Kingdom; the Unwin Fishers apparently purchased a flower piece from Père Tanguy, Van Gogh's unofficial dealer, some time before Tanguy's death in 1894, and Mrs Ethel

fig.40 *The Louis XVI Salon, the Potter Residence, 1350 Lake Shore Drive, Chicago, c. 1900*

Sutro, while studying in Paris in 1893–4, bought 'Le Restaurant Carrel à Arles'.[110] Even after 1900, although there were individual collectors in Britain, no cluster of like-minded and similarly committed individuals emerged until some fifteen years after such a group had been established in Winterthur. Sir Hugh Lane started to collect in 1905, and the Davies sisters embarked upon a spectacular phase of acquisition in 1912, on the advice of Hugh Blaker, buying works by Manet, Renoir and two views of Venice by Monet to form the basis of an outstanding collection of Impressionist and Post-Impressionist works which they ultimately bequeathed to the National Museum of Wales, Cardiff.[111] Finally, there was Michael Sadler, civil servant and eventually Vice-Chancellor of Leeds University, who, during a visit to Paris in 1910 had admired the work of Monet, Sisley, Renoir, Manet and Rodin. The following autumn he commissioned the dealer John Nevill of the Stafford Gallery to search out in Paris on his behalf works by Cézanne and Gauguin. Nevill returned with Cézanne's *Maison abandonnée* and Gauguin's *Vision après le sermon*, *L'Esprit veille*, a self-portrait and one Tahitian pastel [fig.41].[112]

Britain, like Switzerland, lacked any institutions which could give public credence to modern art, and no modern French works were seen on the walls of a national institution until 1917. In part this was due to constraints imposed upon both the National Gallery, which could not purchase any works by living artists, and on its subsidiary, the Tate Gallery, whose acquisitions were restricted solely to works by British artists. Hence, when in 1905 Frank Rutter recommended the purchase by the National Gallery of a work by Monet, the suggestion was rejected by the Trustees, and a

Boudin acquired instead. It was only in 1917 that the National Gallery finally acceded to the posthumous wish of Sir Hugh Lane, against significant opposition voiced by certain Trustees, that a selection of his collection be loaned to the Gallery. The real change in the public fortunes of French Impressionism and Post-Impressionism was not fully to be realised until ten years later when Samuel Courtauld completed the final purchases of major Impressionist and Post-Impressionist works to be housed in the Tate Gallery.[113]

In France official acceptance of Impressionism had initially been slow. The State purchased its first Impressionist work, a painting by Sisley, in 1888.[114] This was followed by the acquisition of a Renoir in 1892,[115] a reluctance to place Manet's *Olympia* in the Louvre and its consequent relegation to the Musée du Luxembourg in 1894, and disputes leading to the final acceptance in 1897 of the Caillebotte Bequest after three years of interminable negotiation. Yet, in 1900, the inclusion of works by the Impressionists in the Exposition Universelle was sanctioned by the State, and thereafter the fortunes of avant-garde art in the public domain improved. Two important bequests of Impressionist works were accepted before 1912, that of Moreau-Nelaton in 1906[116] and that of Comte Camondo in 1911.[117] The former included such works as Manet's *Déjeuner sur l'herbe* [fig.42], and the latter works by Monet, Renoir, Cézanne and Van Gogh. This more positive situation was enhanced by the fact that two successive directors of the Musée du Luxembourg were strong advocates of modern French art: Léonce Bénédite (director 1892–1925)[118] and Louis Hautecœur (director from 1930).[119]

Germany likewise experienced the emergence of a relatively strong institutional base to complement collecting activities. To be sure, there were private collectors, for example the painter Max Liebermann, who had begun to collect Impressionist works in the early 1890s, followed by individuals such as Oskar Schmitz (1901), Harry Graf Kessler (1905), Karl Osthaus (1906), Carl Sternheim (1908) and Paul von Mendelsohn-Bartholdy (c.1910). Some of these collections were conceived with the intention of making them available to the public, as in the case of the Karl Osthaus collection which became the basis of the Folkwang Museum, Hagen (Essen). This sense of public duty reflects the activity of the Swiss-born Hugo von Tschudi, the director first of the Nationalgalerie, Berlin (1896–1909), and, from 1909 until his death two years later, of the Staatsgemäldegalerie in Munich. His acquisition policy as regards Impressionist and Post-Impressionist works set an example which sanctioned the taste of private individuals and provided a model for other public insti-

fig.41 *Spencer Gore, Gauguins and Connoisseurs at the Stafford Gallery (1911–12; Private collection). An exhibition of works by Cézanne and Gauguin opened at the Stafford Gallery, London, in November 1911. Michael Sadler lent several works to the show. On the wall hang Gauguin's* Manau Tupapau (L'Esprit veille), Christ in the Garden *and* Jacob Wrestling with the Angel.

fig.42 *The Moreau-Nelaton Gallery, Musée du Louvre, 1937, with Manet's* Déjeuner sur l'herbe *and works by Delacroix and Corot.*

tutions to follow. In Berlin, Tschudi purchased Manet's *Dans le serre* in 1896, followed by a Pissarro in 1897, a Monet in 1899 and a Renoir in 1906. After his arrival in Munich, he acquired a Van Gogh and commissioned a Matisse, *Still-Life with Geranium*, in 1910; the year after his death the museum was further enriched by donations from private individuals in his memory.[120] Other museums followed the path laid out by Tschudi: Bremen bought a Degas in 1903 and a Van Gogh (*The Poppy Field*, 1890; F.581) in 1911. Cologne purchased Gauguins in 1909 and 1913; and Frankfurt acquired a Sisley as early as 1899, *Au Bords de la Seine en automne* (1876; D.223); other acquisitions followed in Hamburg, Magdeburg, Mannheim and Stuttgart.[121]

Institutional support in the United States was initially not as extensive as that in Germany. But unlike Switzerland, once museums began to acquire examples of the new French art, their commitment was significantly greater. As in Switzerland, institutional collecting started some two decades after the first major collections of French art had been accumulated. In contrast to Switzerland, however, the catalyst to encourage such acquisitions appears to have been several recently established museums willing to host temporary displays of Impressionist and Post-Impressionist art. Exhibitions in museums or official cultural manifestations were held in the States as early as 1893, when the Columbian Worlds Fair in Chicago had included a section entitled, Foreign Masterpieces owned in the United States. Organised by Sara Hallowell, the friend and adviser of the Chicago collector Mrs Palmer Potter, it consisted of 126 works, the majority of which were admittedly of the Barbizon School; but it also included fourteen Impressionist works – four Monets, three Manets, three Pissarros, two Degas, one Renoir and one Sisley. Three years later the inauguration of the Carnegie International in Pittsburgh at the Carnegie Museum of Art moved this kind of exhibition into a museum. This immense survey of contemporary art included the more establishment French artists, such as Besnard, Cazin, Gérôme and Puvis de Chavannes, as well as Degas with two works and Monet with four paintings, all supplied through Durand-Ruel. At the second International, held in 1897–8, there was the same combination of establishment and avant-garde French art. Impressionist works were again included, from which a painting by Alfred Sisley, *Vue de St Mammes* (1881; D.445) was purchased by the museum and thus became the first Impressionist painting to enter an American public institution. Two years later (1899–1900), the Carnegie International included Cassatt, Degas, Boudin, Monet, Sisley and Pissarro, the latter's *Le Grand Pont, Rouen* finding its way into the museum's permanent collection. In 1905, the recently opened Toledo Museum of Art hosted a major exhibition of Impressionist works. Organised by Durand-Ruel (a formula which he was to repeat in St Louis in 1907 and Pittsburgh in 1908[122]), it included four Cassatts, five Degas, two Manets, thirteen Monets, twelve Renoirs, twelve Pissarros and twelve Sisleys. Critical response was no longer couched in the carping tones which had once greeted the exhibitions mounted by Durand-Ruel and his fellow dealers, Knoedler, Boussod, Valadon & Co. and Cottier in New York and Boston during the 1880s.[123] By the turn of the new century, the combination of the force of private collectors and institutional support encouraged the *Toledo Daily Blade* to declare:

> The galleries on the second floor are a riot of colour, and the walls blazed with the intensity and insistence of nature ... when one has relinquished one's mental hold of the painting to which one has become accustomed, and has approached this new art with a reverence and a mind open to conviction, and when one begins to understand something of the theory of light and colour vibrations, one begins to realise the almost miraculous work these men have done.[124]

Critical response to an exhibition opens up a final, but related formative influence on the establishment and shaping of private collections. Switzerland benefited from serious publications and critical articles providing a new framework within which the Impressionist and Post-Impressionist works could be understood. The provision of a language of mediation for collectors and a wider public for what were perceived to be difficult works was not significantly out of step with other countries outside France, where the framework was fragile. The exception to this was Belgium. Both in Brussels and to a lesser degree in Antwerp, regular temporary exhibitions which included Impressionist and Post-Impressionist works, such as those mounted in Brussels by Les XX (1884–93) and the Libre Esthétique (1894–1913), created a focus for critical response.

In terms of the degree of sophistication of critical response, the United Kingdom lagged well behind France, and even, it could be argued, Switzerland. As Kate Flint has shown,[125] despite the presence of a nucleus of exhibitions showing Impressionist works in the 1880s and of the critical activities of George Moore between 1890 and 1894,[126] it was only after the publication of Wyndham Dewhurst's *Impressionist Painting: Its Genesis and Development* in 1904 that the critical literature moved onto a more serious plane. Richard Muther's book on modern painting, *Geschichte der*

Malerei im XIX. Jahrhundert (1893) was published in translation that same year,[127] and Julius Meier-Graefe's *Modern Art* (the translation of *Entwicklungsgeschichte der modernen Kunst*) four years later. The year 1910 was the *annus mirabilis* in the volume and level of serious critical literature, with the publication of Maurice Denis's article on Cézanne in *The Burlington Magazine* (January–February), Théodore Duret's *Manet and French Impressionism*, Frank Rutter's *Revolution in Modern Art* and, in the December issue of *The Burlington Magazine*, R. Mayer-Reifstahl's 'Vincent van Gogh'. Curiously, despite the fact that this latter article coincided with Roger Fry and Clive Bell's exhibition Manet and the Post-Impressionists at the Grafton Galleries, no dramatic increase in interest in French modern painting can be discerned until the following decade. In the United States the somewhat tardy appearance of serious criticism did not deter enthusiasm for collecting. Thus, apart from a lone article by L. Lejeune on Impressionism, 'The Impressionist School of Painting',

published in *Lippincott's Magazine* in 1879,[128] the almost frantic collecting activity of the following decade tended to be accompanied by generally adverse criticism of the temporary exhibitions held both in New York and Boston. It was only in the early 1890s that the collectors found their taste beginning to be vindicated in the critical press with publications such as Theodore Robinson's study of Monet in 1892.[129]

Switzerland's distinction in collecting Impressionist and Post-Impressionist work lies not so much in its being first in the field. Rather, its importance lies in its initial enthusiasm and acuity of taste for this art and for the way in which it was used by some collectors as a point of departure for widening their interest to encompass subsequent developments in Western as well as classical and non-Western art. In each of these fields, collections of international standing have been established, which redounds to the credit of that country.   [MAS]

1 'Of all the towns of the Swiss Confederation none deserves more praise than the City of Basel and its worthy elders for their great expenditure and diligence in collecting and studying the arts, especially excellent paintings, drawings and the like.' Joachim von Sandrart, *Teutsche Academie*, 1679. Sandrart reported how the elders of the City of Basel saved the Amerbach collection by 'buying it, apparently in 1661, for 9,000 crowns in cash and handing it over to the University, where, together with a world-famous library that boasts an abundance of manuscripts, it can now be enjoyed by all. The jewel of this art treasure consists of twenty original paintings by Holbein, in which his genius and skill are beyond praise.' *Joachim von Sandrarts Academie der Bau-, Bild- und Mahlerey-Künste von 1675, Leben der berühmten Maler, Bildhauer und Baumeister*, ed. A. R. Peltzer, Munich 1925, p.321. Quoted in Christian Geelhaar, *Kunstmuseum Basel, The History of the Paintings Collection and a Selection of 250 Masterworks*, Zurich and Basel 1992, pp.9, 29.

2 'Wie ich aber einstweilen die Sache noch ansehe, scheint mir wenig Aussicht zu sein, dass die Kunst in der Schweiz jemals auf einen grüner Zweig komme, trotz der besten Ausstellungen mit gutem Licht, etc, da das Kunstinteresse im Allgemeinen zu gering ist. Wäre die Schweiz ein grösseres Land, so käme es nicht so darauf an, da sich unter viel Millionen Menschen immer noch genug finden, denen die Kunst und der Besitz von Kunstwerken ein Bedürfnis ist; aber bei uns sind die Häupter dieser Lieben bald gezählt.' Letter from Böcklin to Buchser, who had asked him to participate in the creation of a Swiss art Salon. Quoted in Lukas Gloor, *Von Böcklin zu Cézanne: Die Rezeption des französischen Impressionismus in der Deutschen Schweiz*, Bern 1986, p.34, the fullest discussion on the subject of the reception of the new taste in Switzerland.

3 Unlike most of the other European countries, where academies providing formal artistic training and temporary exhibitions had been in existence for more than a century, Switzerland had no such academic tradition. Yet this lack was also going to help Swiss collectors to be more readily open to new art.

4 The first institution was the Basel Kunsthalle, which was created in 1872.

5 '… da die französische Kunst nicht länger unvertreten bleiben konnte…'. Quoted in Gloor 1986, p.53.

6 'Tout leur est nouveau … Ils ont peur de dire leur opinion, ne voulant pas se blâmer…'. Quoted in Gloor 1986, p.54.

7 H. Wölfflin, 'Arnold Böcklin', in *Basler Jahrbuch*, Basel 1898, pp.218–29; reprinted in H. Wölfflin, *Kleine Schriften (1886-1933)*, Basel 1946, pp.109–18; discussed in Gloor 1986, pp.56–8.

8 Jules Laforgue, 'L'Impressionnisme' (1883), *Mélanges posthumes, Œuvres complètes*, vol.3, Paris 1919, pp.140–1.

9 Albert Aurier, 'Les Isolés: Vincent van Gogh', *Œuvres posthumes*, Paris 1893, p.260; quoted in Richard Shiff, *Cézanne and the End of Impressionism*, Chicago 1984, p.32.

10 '"Modern sein", ist jetzt, am Schluss des 19. Jahrhunderts die Parole'; quoted in Gloor 1986, p.65.

11 Meier-Graefe also organized the major Impressionist exhibition at the Vienna Sezession in January/February 1903, bearing the title 'Entwicklung des Impressionismus in Malerei und Plastik' which follows the same developmental model as the book. See Kenworth Moffett's *Meier-Graefe as Art Critic*, Volume 19 in *Studien zur Kunst des 19. Jahrhunderts*, Munich 1973.

12 See Gloor 1986, p.68.

13 'Wir hier in Zürich und in der Schweiz kennen diese Künstler nur durch die Werke von Amiet und Giacometti… Wir möchten die Originale, die echten Franzosen selbst sehen! Schon lange ist das unser Wunsch, unser lebhafter Wunsch und namentlich der unserer Künstler.' Quoted in Gloor 1986, p.97.

14 'Wie würde er uns, teilweise wenigstens, überrascht, selbst verblüfft haben, wenn uns die Amiet und Giacometti nicht längst an ungebrochene, schmetternde Farbklänge gewöhnt hätten – unsere Erzieher zu van Gogh.' *Neue Züricher Zeitung*, 24 November 1908; quoted in Gloor 1986, p.98.

15 Léonce Bénédite played an important role in the first two decades of the 20th century in proselytising French modern art abroad. He forged cultural links between France and Switzerland; in 1924 he organised the counterpart of the Basel Kunsthalle exhibition of 1906 for the Musée du Luxembourg, Paris, entitled Exposition de l'Art suisse du XVème au XIXème siècle (de Holbein à Hodler). The exhibition included 224 objects, among which were some of the most important Holbein paintings in Swiss collections. The reception given to Hodler was somewhat muted.

16 See Koella pp.59–60 and Eva Maria Preiswerk-Lösel pp.88–96 in Luxembourg, *'Luxe, Calme et volupté, Regards sur le Post-Impressionnisme, Collectionneurs à Winterthur et Baden au début du XXᵉ siècle*, Casino Luxembourg, 1995. See as well Florens Deuchler in Baden, *Carl Montag, Maler und Kunstvermittler (1880-1956)*, Stiftung 'Langmatt' Sidney und Jenny Brown, 17 June–31 October 1992, including essays by Rudolf Koella, Georges Duplain, Lukas Gloor, and Eva-Maria Preiswerk-Lösel.

17 Letter from Wartmann to Bernheim-Jeune, Paris, 18 November 1913; quoted in Gloor 1986, p.319.

18 Eugène Boudin, *Laveuses au bord de la Touques* (1895), and Paul-Desiré Trouillebert, *Paysage au bord d'une rivière* (c.1870), both bought for 500 francs from Georges Bernheim, 29 October 1896.

19 Rudolf Koella, 'Winterthur: a Prime Example of Art Collection in Switzerland', in Luxembourg 1995, p.61.

20 Julius Meier-Graefe apparently played a role in the debate which eventually forced the old board to step down. See Rudolf Koella, 'Der Aufbruch in die Moderne', in *Geschichte des Kunstvereins Winterthur seit seiner Gründung 1848*, Winterthur 1990, p.109.

21 See Koella, in Luxembourg 1995, p.57.

22 'Imaginez une histoire vivante de l'art français et qui serait composée dans un petit coin de Suisse, un jardin où se trouverait quelques-unes des plus belles fleurs de notre peinture, une somme de Beauté dans une ambiance sympathique, faite de calme et de recueillement. Ici, ce sont les peintres et parmi eux plus spécialement ceux du XIXᵉ siècle.' Courthion 1926, pp.1–2.

23 Viau continued to collect after these sales, assembling another vast collection, some of which was sold in 1930 and some posthumously between 1942 and 1948. An entry on Viau is included in Sophie Monneret, *L'Impressionnisme et son époque*, vol.3, Paris 1980, pp.49–50.

24 See Florens Deuchler, 'Zur Sammlungsgeschichte der "Langmatt"', *Die französischen Impressionisten und ihre Vorläufer, Sammlungskataloge*, vol.1, Baden 1990, pp.20–1.

25 Ibid., p.17.

26 See Eva-Maria Preiswerk-Lösel, 'Winterthur Collectors in Baden: Sidney and Jenny Brown at the Villa Langmatt', in Luxembourg 1995, pp. 91–3.

27 Hahnloser is the author of the first significant monograph on Vallotton, in 1936, as well as earlier articles about him in 1926, 1927 and 1928. Hahnloser laments the lack of attention that Vallotton received in his native Switzerland in 1931 in *Das Werk*, in response to an article by H. Ganz in the *Neue Züricher Zeitung*. It is worth noting that Julius Meier-Graefe also wrote a monograph on Vallotton, published in Berlin in 1898.

28 'Vallotton à qui nous devons le portrait de Mme Hahnloser est toujours sec, exact. Il y a des passages magnifiques… mais, par contre, nous n'y trouvons rien pour plaire, rien de choisi ni d'ajouté. Il y a chez Vallotton un défaut total d'imagination et de fantaisie. C'est la peinture pauvre d'un trop grand observateur: beaucoup de science et peu d'art.' Courthion 1926, p. 66.

29 'In seltener Generosität regte uns Vallotton an, Bilder seiner Kommilitonen zu erwerben, und begeistert half er mit bei der Wahl der ersten Bonnard, Vuillard und Roussel. Nun erst sahen wir, wie zu unrecht die Kritik Vallottons Schaffen in einen Gegensatz gesetzt hat zu jenem seines Freundeskreises…' Hedy Hahnloser, in *Die Hauptwerke der Sammlung Hahnloser Winterthur*, Kunstmuseum Lucerne, 1940, p. 7.

30 'Die Erneuerung unserer heimischen Kunst kam, wie diejenige in den meisten Ländern, aus Paris. Giovanni Giacometti bewies dies als einer der ersten, als er den grossen Impressionisten die Geheimnisse ihres Schaffens ablauschte. Er war es, der uns in der Schweiz begeistert von Cézanne sprach, prophetisch das Licht voraussagend, das von diesem Stern ausgehen werde. Leider hatten wir erst später den Mut, dieser Botschaft nachzuleben.' Hedy Hahnloser, in Lucerne 1940, p. 6.

31 'Der Reichtum der Einheit von Rot und Grün war mein einziger Gegenstand, meine ganze Seele… Die Farbe ist die Mutter ihrer selbst, die Farbe ist auch die Mutter der sichtbaren Linie, die Farbe endlich ist auch die Mutter der sichtbaren Fläche und des sichtbaren Raumes. Allen bildenden Künsten ist Eines gemeinsam: das Auge, das in der reinen Farbe sein Glück findet.' Oskar Miller, 'Mein Verhältnis zur heutigen Malerei', *Wissen und Leben*, vol. 3, 1908–9, pp. 460–73, here citing pp. 465 and 470.

32 See the auction catalogue, *Sammlung Richard Kisling*, Zurich, G. & L. Bollag, 18 November 1929.

33 The Meyer-Fierz collection was dissolved at auction 13 July 1926, Frederick Muller & Cie, Amsterdam.

34 See the collection catalogue, Hans-Joachim Müller, *NAFEA, The Rudolf Staechelin Collection Basel*, Basel 1991, with contributions by Christian Geelhaar, Franz Meyer, Simon de Pury and Ruedi Staechelin.

35 See Christian Geelhaar, 'Best buy quality has always been my opinion', in Müller, *NAFEA*, p. 171. Geelhaar indicates that it was exhibited at the Kunsthaus Zurich in November 1914, no. 43.

36 One might compare his relatively conservative choices of Picassos with those purchased at around 1920 in Lausanne by the German G. F. Reber, embracing the Spaniard's work in an encyclopedic manner. See D. Kosinski, 'G. F. Reber: collector of Cubism', *The Burlington Magazine*, vol. CXXXII, no. 1061, August 1991, pp. 519–31.

37 This 'September-Ausstellung' replaced an exhibition which had been planned with Josef Müller and which would have featured his collection. The exhibition travelled to Bern after the Basel venue.

38 See Kosinski 1991 (*op. cit.*), p. 524, concerning Einstein, Meier-Graefe and non-European aspects of Reber's collection.

39 See Koella, in Luxembourg 1995, p. 59.

40 PV. 447; see Gloor 1986, pp. 176–7.

41 See Koella, 'Der Aufbruch in die Moderne' (*op. cit.*), p. 120; and Koella, 'Das gloriose Jahrzehnt', in *Das gloriose Jahrzehnt, Französische Kunst 1910–1920 aus Winterthurer Besitz*, exh. cat. Kunstmuseum Winterthur, 22 January–1 April 1991, p. 20.

42 'Renoir war der erste, der die bedenkliche soziale Seite der modernen Kunst, die "splendid isolation" des Individualismus, durchschaute und sich, soweit das einem Menschen unserer Zeit möglich ist, von dem Ich lossagte, um zu der Allgemeinheit zu gehen.' Meier-Graefe, 'Renoir im Rückblick', *Berliner Tageblatt*, no. 506, 25 October 1928; reprinted in *Grundstoff der Bilder*, Munich 1959, p. 194; here as quoted by Kenworth Moffett, *Meier-Graefe as Art Critic*, vol. 19 in *Studien zur Kunst des 19. Jahrhunderts*, Munich 1973, p. 90. Meier-Graefe was also the author of a monograph on Renoir first released in 1911 and re-edited in 1929. According to Moffett, Meier-Graefe had attempted to launch a Renoir exhibition in Dresden in 1897, a project which, however, was rejected as too radical.

43 See Gloor 1986, pp. 136–7.

44 'Bei den Impressionisten ist Alles tot, nur das Licht lebt; bei Böcklin lebt jedes Blümchen, jedes Element ein Eigenleben und Alles stimmt harmonisch zum Ganzen.' Karl Scheffler, 'Monet und Böcklin', *Zukunft*, vol. 35, no. 4, 1901, p. 346.

45 Fritz Ostini, *Arnold Böcklin*, Bielefeld and Leipzig 1904, pp. 2–3.

46 Various exhibitions from the turn of the century may be cited: the Secession exhibitions in Berlin and Vienna, the Libre Esthétique in Brussels, the Carnegie Annual in Pittsburgh, etc. In this regard see Donald E. Gordon, *Modern Art Exhibitions 1900–1916*, Munich 1974.

47 'Die französische Malerei existiert nicht mehr; an ihrer Stelle ist eine ganz neue Malerei mit ganz neuen Auffassungen entstanden; es genügt, die impressionistische Malerei, eine wahre Neger- und Mongolenkunst, mit der alten französischen Malerei zu vergleichen, um sich den geistigen Rückschritt klar zu machten… Sehen wir doch schon in Deutschland eine grosse Schar begeisterter Impressionisten, selbstverständlich unter orientalischen Führern.' Alexander von Senger, 'Betrachtungen über die französischen Impressionisten, Rückblick auf die Oktober-Ausstellung im Kunsthaus', *Wissen und Leben*, vol. 2, 1908–9, no. 6, pp. 241–5 (here pp. 244, 245). Von Senger draws on the work of the French social anthropologist Lapouge. See also Gloor 1986, pp. 119–27.

48 Hans Schuler, 'Impressionismus. Eine Entgegnung', which followed in *Wissen und Leben*, vol. 2, 1908–9, no. 7, pp. 292–6.

49 'A la race nous opposons la nation; à la haine, la civilisation; à la nature aveugle, la conscience; c'est, dans l'univers physique, la création glorieuse de l'homme; c'est dans la nuit des servitudes, le chemin qui monte à la lumière et à la liberté.' Ernest Bovet, 'Réflexions d'un homo alpinus', *Wissen und Leben*, vol.2, 1908–9, no.7, pp.296–9 (here p.299). Two additional articles followed: 'Kunstgedanken eines vollständigen Laien' by Dr F. Fick and 'Ein Wort der Entgegnung', by Dr Albert Baur, the editor of the magazine; and in the next issue yet another article by Von Senger, 'Impressionismus, eine Gegenentgegnung'.

50 'Leider hat ein grosser Teil der deutschen Nation seit Schiller und Goethe die Sehkraft eingebüsst, aber nicht nur blind, sondern charakterlos war es, wie diese gebildeten Deutschen so schnell von Böcklins Kunst zu derjenigen einiger französischer Impressionisten bekehrt waren, von denen ihnen diejenigen am meisten Eindruck machten, welche sich eines ehrlichen Naturalismus schämten, und durch allerlei Pinseltänzereien freie Erfindung und Phantasie vorzutäuschen suchen.' Albert Welti, 'Meier-Graefe und Van Gogh', *Wissen und Leben*, vol.4, 1910–11, no.11, pp.789–90.

51 'Eine andere Kunstanschauung, die des Impressionismus, hat ihren typischen Schweizervertreter in der Person des Kuno Amiet. Die Impressionisten stellten koloristische Effekte über die Bedeutung des Inhaltes, ja selbst über die reale Wahrheit. Kuno Amiet ist der Agent des fix und fertig in die Schweiz importierten französischen Impressionismus, der aber seither längst international geworden ist…' Dr Johannes Winkler, *Mißstände in der schweizerischen Kunstpflege*, Bern, 31 August 1911, p.9. Concerning Winkler, see Gloor 1986, p.284, n.129.

52 H.G. [Hans Graber], 'Hodler, die Schweiz und Deutschland', newspaper clipping in Press Album of the Basler Kunstverein, Archive of the Basel Kunsthalle. See another article dated 10 December 1913, as well as an ironic commentary by Hans Oehler from February 1914, 'Heiterer Nachtrag zur Kunstdebatte im Ständerat'.

53 'Zu den Kunstdebatten in den Eidgenössischen Räten', in the Press Album of the Basler Kunstverein, Archive of the Basel Kunsthalle.

54 'Betrachtet man die Ausstellung der Impressionisten als Ganzes, so wird es einem schwer zu verstehen, wie viele Leute einst fast allgemein als revolutionär oder gar als verrückt verschreien und ihre Ausstellungen als Lachkabinette benützt werden konnten. Für uns Heutige haben viele Bilder gar nichts Aufregendes mehr, ja wir empfinden sie schon fast als altmeisterlich, als etwas Historisches. Diese Tatsache sollte die Bekämpfer und Belacher moderner Malerei, wie der Hodlers u.a. doch etwas nachdenklich stimmen.' Hans Graber, 'Die Oktoberausstellung in der Basler Kunsthalle, Ausstellung französischer Malerei des 19.Jahrhunderts seit Courbet', *Basler Nachrichten*, 19 and 22 October 1913. A cautious appraisal of Cubism and Futurism is to be found as late as 1940 in Hedy Hahnloser's text to the exhibition of her collection in Bern.

55 This is the title of an article by Hans Oehler, in *Feuilleton*, 1916, in the Press Album of the Basler Kunstverein, Archive of the Basel Kunsthalle. Oehler ironically comments on the chauvinistic celebrations of Hodler, citing in particular Maeder: 'In Hodler begrüssen wir und feiern wir den ersten grossen absolut und ausschliesslich schweizerischen Künstler… Er hat die Tyrannie des fremden Einflusses überwunden und das für ihn, für den Ausbruch seiner Persönlichkeit geeignete erworben.'

56 In this regard, see Lukas Gloor, 'Kunst als Propaganda im Ersten Weltkrieg, Carl Montag als "Ambassadeur de l'art français"', in *Carl Montag, Maler und Kunstvermittler (1880–1956)*, exh.cat. Baden 1992, pp.19–26.

57 Hedy Hahnloser, 'Vorbilder der schweizerischen Kunst', *Nationalzeitung*, Basel, 18 August 1919, no.364, n.p.

58 'Schliesslich hat der Weltkrieg und das wirtschaftliche Chaos, das darauf folgte und dessen Ende wir noch nicht erblicken können, die naive Sammelfreudigkeit gedämpft und das unsichere Gefühl, was die kommenden Jahre uns in wirtschaftlicher, politischer und kultureller Beziehung noch bringen werden, tritt hindernd in den Weg.' Georg Reinhart, *Katalog meiner Sammlung*, Winterthur 1922.

59 'Nach dem Krieg trat eine neue Käuferschicht in Erscheinung: die Industriellen. Man kann wohl sagen, dass es gegenwärtig keinen grossen Namen aus der Schweizer Industrie gibt, der nicht auch im Reich der Sammler einen guten Klang hat: Sulzer, Dubied, Dübi, Abegg, Stoll, Rom, Stierlin, Firmenich, Junod, von Hirsch, Rupf, Rosengart, Staehlin, Sydney Brown sind Namen, die nicht nur an Lokomotiven, Nähmaschinen, Uhren, pharmazeutische Präparate, Schokolade, Schuhe, Parfums, Grossbanken oder einen anderen Zweig von Handel und Industrie denken lassen, sondern auch an Bilder von Courbet, Corot, Daumier, Delacroix, Manet, Cézanne, Renoir, Gauguin, van Gogh, Rouault, Picasso und Klee…'. Cabanne, *Die Geschichte grosser Sammler, Emil Georg Bührle*, 1963, p.165.

60 For example, between 1923 and 1926, Richard Bühler bought seven works by Félix Vallotton from Galerie Paul Vallotton. Guy and Marina Ducrey, *La Galerie Paul Vallotton, depuis 1913…*, Lausanne 1988, p.59.

61 See Gloor 1986, p.137.

62 See Gloor 1986, p.299; the sale was published as 'Tableaux modernes, Aquarelles. Collection Fritz Meyer de Zurich [sic]'. Gloor, p.299, n.275.

63 See above.

64 Willy Russ sold back to the Galerie Paul Vallotton, Lausanne, three Renoirs, two Vuillards, a seascape by Courbet, a Daumier, a Van Gogh and a Picasso. See Ducrey 1988, p.58.

65 *Ibid.*, p.59.

66 The other two sons, Hans and Werner, inherited more of their father's musical interests; Stravinsky, for example, was a regular visitor to the family home, Zum Rychenberg.

67 D.528.

68 Cézanne, *Marronnier du Jas de Bouffan*, V.478, was bought from Vollard in April 1912; Gauguin's *Nature morte*, W.287, was bought from Galerie Druet in May 1912; Degas, *Femme aux cheveux roux*, L.528, was bought from Durand-Ruel in 1912; Renoir, *Femme en blanc*, was bought from Durand-Ruel in October 1912 (see G. Reinhart, *Katalog meiner Sammlung*, Winterthur 1922, no.32).

69 He bought Corot, *Bretonne allaitant son enfant*, R.1269; Delacroix, *Le Christ sur le Lac de Génézareth*, R.1217; for the works by Daumier and Goya, see Reinhart, *Katalog*, 1922, nos.42 and 43.

70 Reinhart, *Katalog*, 1922.

71 He apparently studied the works of Dürer, Rembrandt, Rowlandson and Constable in the British Museum Print Room. See Lisbeth Stähelin, 'Introduction', *Oskar Reinhart Collection, 'Am Römerholz'*, Winterthur, n.d.

72 For fuller information on Oskar Reinhart and his collection, see *ibid*.

73 Fritz Nathan, *Erinnerungen aus meinem Leben*, Zurich 1965, p.83.

74 Michael Sadleir, *Michael Ernest Sadler, (Sir Michael Sadler KCSI), 1861–1943: A Memoir by his Son*, London 1949, pp.233–4.

75 Gloor 1986, p.174.

76 Nathan, *Erinnerungen*, p.82.

77 *Ibid*. p.90.

78 *Ibid.*, p.92.

79 *Ibid.*, p.95. These auctions included the stock and private collection of the dealer Paul Rosenberg. Nathan claims that he was operational in the restitution of Rosenberg's collection of drawings in 1947; see Nathan, *Erinnerungen*, p.105.

80 Bührle acquired from Aktuaryus, Zurich, in 1944 Monet, *Le Déjeuner*.

81 1878; RW.271.

82 1904–6; V.802.

83 1889; F.724.

84 1881; W.536.

85 1881; RW.258.

86 1880; D.324.

87 1873.

88 1889; F.633.

89 1888; F.481.

90 1901; W.598.

91 See *The Passionate Eye: Impressionist and other Master Paintings from the E.G. Bührle Collection*, exh.cat. National Gallery of Art, Washington DC;... Royal Academy of Arts, London, 1989–90.

92 1901; W.607.

93 *c*.1903.

94 Pissarro, *La Route de Versailles à Louveciennes*, bought 1952; Pissarro, *La Route de Pontoise à Osny*, bought 1952; Manet, *La Sultane*, bought 1952; Toulouse-Lautrec, *Les Deux Amies*, bought 1954.

95 Stoll also collected sculpture, and in the 1950s extended his collection to include oriental art. For further information on Stoll, see, *Katalog der Sammlung Arthur Stoll*, Zurich and Stuttgart 1961.

96 This collector started to collect in the 1930s, making his first significant purchases around 1933. His work as a correspondent for a Basel chemical company took him abroad frequently to Paris, London and New York.

97 'Chefs-d'œuvre dans les collections Suisse-Romande', Musée de l'Hermitage, Lausanne 1984.

98 *Schwabischer Merkur*, 15 June 1911; quoted in Rudolf Koella, 'Winterthur: A Prime Example of Art Collection in Switzerland', in Luxembourg 1995, p.65.

99 Ambroise Vollard, *Souvenirs d'un marchand de tableaux*, Paris 1937, p.382.

100 See Gloor 1986, pp.133–4.

101 See Sadleir, *op. cit*.

102 See Frances Weitzenhofer, 'The earliest American collections of Monet', in J. Rewald and F. Weitzenhofer (ed.), *Aspects of Monet*, pp.72–91, esp. pp.79, 80. Fuller also organised the first one-man exhibition of Monet at the Union League Club, New York, in February 1891. Hung in the club concurrently with another exhibition of old and modern masters, the exhibition included thirty-four paintings by Monet, lent by Catholina Lambert, Albert Spencer, Alden Wyman Kingman, James Sutton, Cyrus Lawrence, Erwin Davis, William Andrews, Alfred Pope and Fuller himself; there were also loans from Durand-Ruel and Boussod & Valadon. Fuller wrote the brochure accompanying the exhibition, praising Monet for his 'truthfulness' and hailing him as the undisputed leader of the 'school of Naturalistic Art'.

103 Frances Weitzenhofer, *The Havemayers: Impressionism comes to America*, New York 1986.

104 See George Harvey, *Henry Clay Frick: The Man*, New York 1936, pp.337–8.

105 See Beverly Whitney White, *French Painters, Russian Collectors. Shchukin, Morozov and Modern French Art 1890–1914*, London 1983, revised 1994; especially Appendix 3, 'The Sergey Shchukin Collection', pp.269–83; and Appendix 4, 'The Ivan Morozov Collection', pp.285–99.

106 See Geneviève Lacambre, 'Introduction', *Les Oubliés du Caire: Chefs-d'œuvre des musées du Caire*, exh.cat. Musée d'Orsay, Paris 1994. The main thrust of the collecting in Egypt of French 19th-century art, including Impressionism and Post-Impressionism, was during the inter-war years. The taste for such art was shaped as much by the desire to make a political gesture of defiance against the British as it was to express an affinity with modernity. Khalil bought Impressionist works from 1919 in Paris from Durand-Ruel, Bernheim-Jeune and later from Georges Petit; by 1928, at the Exposition d'Art français au Caire 1827–1917, Khalil was able to lend fifty works, including those by Corot, Millet, Courbet, Monet, Renoir, Pissarro, Sisley, Gauguin and Toulouse-Lautrec. Moïse Levy de Benzion bought primarily through Bernheim-Jeune during the 1920s; after his death the collection was auctioned on 14 March 1947 at his house at Zamalek, Cairo. Youssef Kamel bought his first French painting, a Delacroix flower piece, from Bernheim-Jeune in 1919; his collection was given to the Guezireh Museum in 1952.

107 Most notable was the collection of Wilhelm Hansen (1868–1936) who, from 1916, together with another important collector, Herman Heilbuth, and the auctioneers Winkel and Magnussen, set about 'making good and outstanding [French] art available in Scandinavia'. Despite having to sell a considerable number of works in 1922 (several purchased by the Ny Carlsberg Foundation), Hansen continued to purchase major French 19th-century works, donating them to the State on his death. This donation forms the Ordrupgaard Collection, Copenhagen.

108 See William S. Johnston, 'Alfred Sisley and the Early Interest in Impressionism in America 1865–1913', *Alfred Sisley*, exh.cat. Royal Academy of Arts, London 1992, pp.57–8.

109 See Weitzenhofer, *op.cit.*, pp.78–9.

110 See Douglas Cooper, *The Courtauld Collection of Paintings, Drawings, Engravings and Sculpture*, London 1954, pp.60–2. Identified as 'F.540' by Cooper, this title does not correspond with a work of that title or subject. For three other restaurant subjects, F.467, F.1508, F.1519, none of them list 'Sutro' as an early owner of the work.

...

111 See J. Steegman, ed., *Catalogue of the Gwendoline Davies Bequest*, National Museum of Wales, Cardiff 1952.

112 Michael Sadleir, *Michael Ernest Sadler, 1861–1943*, London 1949, pp.228–31. While in Paris in 1910, Sadler visited Durand-Ruel's gallery to view works by Daumier and the Impressionists. At that point in the evolution of his taste he concluded that generally the Impressionists (i.e. Pissarro, Sisley and Rafaëlli) were 'too much like one another' but that Manet and Monet 'stood out from the rest' (p.228). Sadler's commitment to the new art was also demonstrated in his willingness to back John Nevill for the exhibition which Nevill put on at the Stafford Gallery in 1912.

113 See *Impressionism for England. Samuel Courtauld as Patron and Collector*, Courtauld Institute Galleries, London 1994, pp.10–12.

114 *Matin de septembre*, c.1887, D.692, Musée des Beaux-Arts, Agen; see *Alfred Sisley* (op.cit.), pp.272–3.

115 *Jeunes Filles au piano*, Musée d'Orsay, Paris.

116 See V. Pomerède, *Etienne Morean-Nelaton, un collectionneur peintre ou un peintre collectionneur*, Paris 1988; and *Les Donateurs du Louvre*, exh.cat. Musée du Louvre/Réunion des Musées nationaux, Paris 1989, p.277.

117 *Les Donateurs du Louvre*, p.163.

118 Léonce Bénédite had a significant impact on the propagation of a taste for French modern art outside France. Apart from organising the Exposition d'Art français for Basel Kunsthalle in 1906, Bénédite also organised an exhibition at the Musée du Luxembourg in 1924 entitled Exposition de l'Art suisse du XVème au XIXème siècle (de Holbein à Hodler). He also advised the wealthy Japanese collector, Kojio Matsujata, whose collection formed the basis of the National Museum of Western Art, Tokyo.

119 Louis Hautecœur became Directeur des Beaux-Arts du Royaume d'Egypte in December 1927. He remained in post, encouraging the developing taste for French art in Egypt until 1930, when he was recalled to Paris to become director of the Musée du Luxembourg.

120 See Cooper, *op.cit.*, pp.70–1.

121 *Ibid.*

122 See Weitzenhofer, *op.cit.*

123 See Johnston, *op.cit.*, pp.56–9.

124 Quoted in K. Brettell, 'In Search of Modern French Painting', in *Impressionism: Selections from five American Museums*, exh. cat., Pittsburgh, Minneapolis, Kansas City, St Louis, Toledo, 1989, New York 1989, p.19.

125 See Kate Flint, ed., *Impressionists in England. The Critical Reception*, London, Boston, Melbourne and Henley 1984.

126 *Ibid.*, p.65.

127 *The History of Modern Painting*, 3 vols., London 1904.

128 Vol.24, pt.2, 1879, pp.720–7.

129 'Claude Monet', *The Century Magazine*, 44 (September 1892).

CATALOGUE

MARY CASSATT

PITTSBURGH, USA, 22 May 1844 – CHÂTEAU BEAUFRESNE, BEAUVAIS, 14 June 1926

The daughter of a rich Pittsburgh businessman of French ancestry, Mary Cassatt studied at the Pennsylvania Academy of Fine Arts in Philadelphia. She travelled in Europe before settling in Paris in 1874 and showing a work in the Salon of that year. In 1877 she met Degas, who became a life-long friend and introduced her to the Impressionists, with whom she exhibited in 1879, 1880, 1881 and 1886. An acute observer, she took as her theme intimate scenes of domestic life. An exhibition of Japanese prints in 1891 led her to adopt a clearer, more emphatic outline which she applied to her print-making and to her work in pastel. Her financial independence allowed her to support the Impressionists in the early years, and she also promoted the collecting of Impressionist paintings in the United States.

Work by Mary Cassatt has never figured significantly in Swiss collections. It did not appear regularly in the early exhibitions of Impressionism held after 1908 and, in the preface to the catalogue accompanying the 1917 Zurich Kunsthaus exhibition, Französische Kunst des XIX. und XX. Jahrhunderts, Maurice Denis discusses the group of artists surrounding Manet – Monet, Pissarro, Sisley, Renoir, Degas, Berthe Morisot – without mentioning her name. Her work was not included in that exhibition.

However, as early as 19 March 1910, Carl Montag proposed two works by Cassatt, L'Enfant en bleu and Jeunes filles brodant, for consideration by Sidney and Jenny Brown. They chose the pastel, L'Enfant en bleu, possibly because it was significantly cheaper than Jeunes filles brodant. At the same time Montag brought a Berthe Morisot to their attention, but they decided against purchase, and neither a Morisot nor another Cassatt entered their collection. More recently, works by Cassatt have entered those collections which have also favoured works by Degas, for example the Fondation Rau.

1 Louise Nursing her Child

Louise allaitant son enfant; c. 1895
pastel on paper, 72.4 x 53.4 cm
signed lower left
Fondation Rau pour le Tiers-Monde, Zurich

Cassatt never achieved the brilliant, radical effects with pastel that were the hallmark of Edgar Degas, her lifelong friend. However, she worked extensively in the medium, and was able to realise its full range of effects, from subtly brushed-in areas to dense zones of colour to create velvety textures. Whereas Degas explored the interplay between surface and volume in his pastels of bathers and dancers of the 1880s and '90s [see cat. 17], Cassatt's enduring respect for the Old Masters led her to define the human form with clarity, stressing outline and tonal modelling.

From early in her career, Cassatt had used friends and members of her family as models. Here she records Louise Fissier de Fresnaux nursing her child. It is one of a large group of mother-and-child subjects which Cassatt also explored in a series of prints which combine etching, dry-point and aquatint to produce a visual equivalent of Japanese colour woodblock prints.

PAUL CÉZANNE

AIX-EN-PROVENCE, 19 January 1839 – AIX-EN-PROVENCE, 23 October 1906

The son of a banker, Cézanne trained at the Ecole des Beaux-Arts in Aix and copied the Old Masters in the Musée Granet. In 1861 he joined his childhood friend Emile Zola in Paris and attended the free Académie Suisse where he met Pissarro. At this date he studied the work of Delacroix and Courbet, but thereafter Pissarro became his mentor. Cézanne exhibited at the first Impressionist exhibition (1874). He abandoned the imaginative subject-matter and heavy impasto technique of his early style for *plein air* landscape painting and still-lifes, stating that his aim was to 'do Poussin over again from nature': that is, to create lucid, monumental compositions out of transient nature, thereby sowing the seeds for the destruction of Impressionism. He also painted figure subjects, such as the *Card Players*, endowing them with the permanence and structure of a still-life, and made portraits throughout his career; towards the end of his life he adopted the medium of watercolour.

Pioneer Swiss collectors were familiar with the exalted position accorded to Paul Cézanne within the evolution of French art by Julius Meier-Graefe in his book, *Entwicklungsgeschichte der modernen Kunst* (Stuttgart 1904). Furthermore, the work of Swiss avant-garde artists such as Hodler, Amiet and Vallotton, also acquired by these pioneer collectors, had hung beside Cézanne in international exhibitions since 1902. And Carl Montag, the Swiss artist who moved to Paris in 1903, knew two important holdings of Cézanne's work in Paris, those of the collector Dr Georges Viau and the dealer Ambroise Vollard.

Many of the early collections of French Impressionist and Post-Impressionist works in Switzerland included works by Cézanne, notably those of Arthur and Hedy Hahnloser [see cat. 5], Georg Reinhart, Josef Müller and Sidney and Jenny Brown. Between 1908 and 1933, the Browns acquired nine Cézannes, of which five were still-lifes, three landscapes and one a composition of bathers. Six of these were purchased from Vollard, including what was probably the first Cézanne to enter a Swiss collection, *Nature morte: pêches et carafe sur nappe* (c. 1900; V. 739), bought in 1908. Georges Viau sold them a still-life in 1910, Georges Bernheim another still-life in 1913 and Bernheim-Jeune *Maison à Auvers* (c. 1875; V. 143) in 1915. The Browns' first Cézanne was an austere still-life, and the first Cézanne to enter the collection of Josef Müller in 1911 was a brooding portrait of the gardener Vallier (1905–6; V. 717).

Cézanne was included in many of the group exhibitions held after 1908 in Zurich, Basel, Winterthur and Lucerne. A major retrospective of his work was shown at the Kunsthalle Basel from August to October 1936. Such visibility encouraged continued interest in his work among newer collectors such as Oskar Reinhart, who began in 1919, and Emil Georg Bührle. Bührle bought his first Cézanne through Siegfried Rosengart of Lucerne in 1937 (*Mont Ste Victoire*, 1904; V. 802); over the course of the next two decades, he purchased major works by the artist both through Swiss dealers such as Fritz Nathan and other private collectors, such as G. F. Reber of Lausanne, and from galleries in New York.

2 Paul Alexis Reading at Zola's House

La Lecture de Paul Alexis chez Zola; c. 1867
oil on canvas, 52 x 56 cm
V. 118
Private Collection

Both the date and the identification of the figures
in this painting have been questioned. If the title
is correct, the work shows Paul Alexis, Cézanne's
childhood friend from Aix-en-Provence, in the
company of the writer and critic Emile Zola, in the
latter's apartment in Paris. Alexis joined Zola in
September 1869. However, the broad handling of the
paint and the presence of the heavy curtain on the
left making reference to Dutch 17th-century interiors,
notably Gerrit Dou's *Dropsical Woman* which Cézanne
saw in 1866, suggest an earlier date, *c.* 1867, for the
painting, but since Alexis was not in Paris at that time,
it has been suggested that the second figure could be
a self-portrait of Cézanne. Zola and the artist remained
close friends after they had moved to Paris in 1858 and
1861 respectively and, throughout the subsequent two
decades, Zola was to provide Cézanne with critical
support.

3 The House of Dr Gachet, Auvers

La Maison du Docteur Gachet, à Auvers; 1873
oil on canvas, 56 x 47 cm
V. 146
Rudolf Staechelin Family Foundation

Dr Gachet was a homeopathic practitioner and
amateur printmaker resident at Auvers-sur-Oise. He
befriended the Impressionists, collected their works,
and harboured Vincent van Gogh during his final
months in Auvers prior to his suicide in July 1890.

In 1872 Cézanne moved to Auvers. Here he
renewed his friendship with Camille Pissarro who had
settled in nearby Pontoise after his sojourn in London
to escape the Franco–Prussian War. Over the next eight
years, Cézanne worked in front of nature, frequently
in close collaboration with Pissarro. While Cézanne
lightened his palette, together they forged styles which
sought to give greater unity and coherence to a given
scene. For Cézanne this involved an analysis of the
constituent parts of a landscape which would then
be reduced to essential volumetric forms described
through systematically applied, directional brushwork.
In the work shown here the analysis has been applied
to the simple blocking-in of the doctor's house, the
other buildings, the sweep of the road and the rising
ground crowned with trees in the centre of the composition.

In an article of 1904, based on conversations
with Cézanne, Emile Bernard rightly stated that it was
Pissarro who persuaded Cézanne to devote himself
solely to the study of nature: 'It is at Auvers, next to
Pissarro, that he embarks upon the simplifying creation
of the sincere, so naïvely learned art which he has
continued to present us with ever since ...'

cat. 2

cat. 3

4   The Sea at Estaque

La Mer à l'Estaque; 1876
oil on canvas, 42 x 59 cm
'signed' lower right
V. 168
Fondation Rau pour le Tiers-Monde, Zurich

This landscape shows a view across the rooftops of Estaque to the Gulf of Marseilles and, in the distance, the Iles de Frioul. Cézanne had first visited the fishing village of Estaque in 1870, when he had fled to avoid being drafted to fight in the Franco–Prussian War. He returned there in 1875 and 1876.

This painting seems to have challenged Cézanne's understanding of the role of colour in the description of light and shade rather than the more 'academic' procedure of 'modelling', that is the representation of light and shade through the application of white and black. In a letter to Pissarro dated 2 July 1876, Cézanne states: 'I have started two little motifs where there is the sea. Red roofs against a blue sea... These are motifs that would be three or four months of work, which I would like to carve out, for the vegetation does not change here. There are the olive trees and the pines which always keep their leaves. The sun here is so shocking that it seems to me that the objects rise up in silhouette not only in black and white, but in blue, red, brown, violet. I may be mistaken but it seems to me that this is the antithesis of modelling'.

5 The Valley of the Arc

La Vallée de l'Arc; 1878–83
oil on canvas, 57 x 72 cm
V. 296
Private Collection

This painting shows a view across the River Arc, which runs westwards past the Mont Ste Victoire through Aix-en-Provence, debouching into the Mediterranean through the Etang de Berre to the west of Marseilles. The viaduct striding across the middle distance carries the railway line from Aix to Marseilles via Gardanne.

Even more than in either *The Sea at Estaque* [cat. 4] or *The House of Dr Gachet, Auvers* [cat. 3], the analysis of forms and the relationship of receding planes in this landscape have been translated into consistently

applied directional brushwork. It has been argued that the greater intensity of the contrasts between light and shade found under a more southerly sun encouraged such analysis and distanced Cézanne's work from that of the Impressionists, notably Renoir and Monet. These two artists did not integrate the experience of southern light into their work until the early 1880s.

6 Médan: The Château and the Village

Médan: château et village; c.1885
oil on canvas, 81 x 65 cm
V. 439
Private Collection, Zurich

Emile Zola, novelist, critic and childhood friend of
Cézanne [see cat. 2], had bought a house in the village of
Médan on the River Seine to the north-west of Paris in
1878. Cézanne stayed for the first time at Médan the
following year and, until the acrimonious termination
of their friendship seven years later, he was to be a
regular visitor. It was there that in 1880 Zola introduced
Cézanne to the young author and critic J.-K. Huysmans,
who subsequently supported Cézanne, writing an
article published in *La Cravache* in 1886.

This work, with its horizontal bands of river, bank,
village, trees and sky, uses a similar compositional
structure to that found in a painting of almost the same
view made c.1880 (Burrell Collection, Glasgow; V. 325).
However, in this earlier view, the handling of the paint
is much heavier and the colours somewhat dense and
sombre. While the presence of pencil outline over
areas of white primed canvas suggests that the present
work might not be finished, the generally lighter
palette and the thinner, almost transparent handling
of colour suggest a date closer to 1885.

7 **Still-Life:**
   Jug and Plate of Pears

Nature morte: pichet et assiette de poires;
1885–90
oil on canvas, 38.5 x 46 cm
V. 609
Collection S

From early in his career Cézanne had found that still-life subjects presented him with a constant source of technical and compositional challenge. While his still-lifes of the 1870s were shown frontally, works of the succeeding decade, such as this one, show the subjects set in deeper, more complex spaces. Such spatial arrangements presented Cézanne with a continual dialogue between the rhythm of line and colour used to define the objects and their volumetric form, both as individual shapes and set within space. It was this interplay between the two- and three-dimensional

that provided a crucial example for a younger generation of artists, notably Paul Gauguin and Emile Bernard, who, in the late 1880s, were seeking to move painting away from naturalist description and towards a more decorative, non-naturalist mode of expression [see cat. 24].

8 Landscape: Forest Scene

Paysage: sous-bois; c. 1895 or later
oil on canvas, 63 x 80 cm
V. 647
Private Collection

Although this work lacks any specific geographic
location, it was probably painted in the vicinity of the
Jas de Bouffan, Cézanne's property outside Aix, which
was a continual source of motifs. The sombre colours,
subtly modulated to create a dominant dark tonality,
and the thickly laid-on paint applied in directional
brushstrokes suggest a date towards the middle of
the 1890s. The monumental nature of this landscape,
with the surface seemingly sculpted as if in bas-relief,
presents parallels with Cézanne's extravagant still-lifes
of the same period.

9 Path from the Mas Jolie
   to the Château Noir

Chemin du Mas Jolie au Château Noir; 1900–2
oil on canvas, 79.5 x 64.5 cm
V. 1527
Beyeler Collection, Basel

The Château Noir lay midway between Aix-en-Provence and Le Tholonet, on the road leading eastward out of Aix towards Mont Ste Victoire. The recently constructed château and its grounds provided Cézanne with a significant number of motifs towards the end of his life.

As in the *Banks of a River* [cat. 10], this painting works on both a two-dimensional and a three-dimensional plane. The regularity of the zones of directional brushwork, punctuated by intermittent blue lines, creates a flat, patterned surface. As blue lines translate into tree trunks, and directional brushwork opens out to indicate a path caught in dappled sunlight, the composition gradually offers up an illusion of space. Yet, as in Cézanne's late still-lifes, the conventional recession of a composition into the depth is overturned by the radiating pattern of directional brushstrokes placed at the focal point. These seem to wrench that point away from the depth and pull it forward to a central position on the front plane. It was the innovative nature of this understanding of space which was identified by Clement Greenberg as the significant quality of Cézanne's late work: 'Only in the last ten or fifteen years of Cézanne's life do pictures whose power is complete as well as striking and original come from his easel with real frequency. Then the means at last fulfils itself. The illusion of depth is constructed with the surface plane more vividly, more obsessively in mind; the facet-planes may jump back and forth between the surface and the images they create, yet they are one with both surface and image' ('Cézanne', in *Art and Culture*, 1961).

10 Banks of a River

Bords d'une rivière; c. 1900–2
oil on canvas, 65 x 81 cm
V. 771
Private Collection

The organisation of the constituent parts of this land-scape – river, reflection, bank, sky – into horizontal bands parallel to the picture plane is reminiscent of the views of Medan made in the early 1880s [see cat. 6] and also prevents any traditional representation of three-dimensional recession. This disregard for representation of depth is reinforced by the laying-in of colour in square blocks, or slabs, of brushwork, creating the effect of a patchwork quilt. In the last six years of his life, Cézanne experimented to see how far the conven-tion of three-dimensional recession in landscape could be dispensed with. In this respect, the painting shown here has much in common with the sequence of views of the Mont Ste Victoire made between 1902 and 1906, the year of Cézanne's death.

EDGAR DEGAS

PARIS, 19 June 1834 – PARIS, 27 September 1917

A member of a French banking family which had settled in Naples in 1789, in 1854 Degas entered the Paris atelier of Lamothe, the pupil of Ingres and Flandrin, moving to the Ecole des Beaux-Arts the following year. From 1856 to 1858 Degas was in Rome, Naples and Florence. He established himself in Paris as a history painter but was increasingly attracted to the literary and artistic avant-garde circle centred around Manet at the Café Guerbois. After 1870, he adopted this group's interest in contemporary subject-matter, which he used as the vehicle for the analysis of space and movement. He exhibited at all eight Impressionist exhibitions from 1874 to 1886.

During the 1880s, he gradually abandoned oil paint and adopted pastel as his favoured medium, although his subject-matter was the same as in the previous decade. After 1890 his eyesight started to fail.

Degas was not collected as enthusiastically by early Swiss collectors as were Renoir, Cézanne, Pissarro and Sisley. The first two works by the artist to enter Swiss collections were bought by Georg Reinhart and Sidney and Jenny Brown in 1912. Reinhart purchased the early painting *Femme aux cheveux roux* (L. 528) from Durand-Ruel on 3 May, and the Browns bought from Vollard in August 1912 the pastel *Etude de nu* (c. 1885; L. 606). Two years later, on 7 February 1914, the Browns acquired their second work, a brooding study of the head of a man (*Portrait d'homme*, before 1856). An indication of the relative lack of widespread interest in Degas is illustrated by the fact that, out of 245 works included in the Zurich exhibition, Französische Kunst des XIX. und XX. Jahrhunderts, held in 1917, only six were by Degas. Furthermore, of these six only two drawings can be firmly identified as having been lent by a Swiss collector, Richard Kisling; the other four were supplied by galleries in Paris.

Between 1918 and 1939, no major exhibition of Degas's work was held in Switzerland. Little interest was shown in his work by the influential group of Winterthur collectors, with the exception of Oskar Reinhart who acquired an important pastel, *Danseuse dans sa loge* (c. 1878–9; L. 529), which had previously been in the Georges Viau collection in Paris.

Another pastel, *Femme sortant du bain* (c. 1895; L. 606) was bought on 9 April 1919 by Gertrud Dübi-Müller of Solothurn from a modest exhibition of some twenty pastels and drawings shown at the Galerie Paul Vallotton, Lausanne. Two years later, Paul Vallotton arranged with Gustav Tanner to mount an exhibition of all of Degas's bronzes at the Tanner Gallery, Zurich. It is unclear how many pieces were actually sold, and to whom. In 1934, Sidney and Jenny Brown added two further works by Degas to their collection. In keeping with their taste for small-scale landscapes by artists such as Boudin and Corot, these were small oil sketches of Italian landscapes.

Although far greater interest was shown in Degas's work after 1945, the sources for his work tended to be international. To be sure, certain émigré gallery owners established in Zurich, such as Nathan and Marianne Feilchenfeldt, handled his work, but when in 1951 and 1952 Emil Georg Bührle came to acquire his major works such as *Mme Camus au piano* (L. 207), *Vicomte Lepic et ses filles* (L. 272) and *Classe de danse* (L. 587), he found them in Paris or the United States. The strength of interest in Degas's work today is witnessed to by number of loans from private collections in Switzerland to two recent exhibitions, at the Fondation Gianadda, Martigny, and at the Kunsthaus, Zurich.

11 Dancer Resting

Danseuse au repos; 1878
pastel on paper, 61 x 56 cm
signed lower left
L. 480
Private Collection

Degas embarked on the theme of ballet dancers around 1870 when a frieze of legs, tutus and arms appears above the musicians in *L'Orchestre de l'Opéra* (c. 1870, Musée d'Orsay, Paris; L. 186). Over the next three decades he was to explore the subject of the ballet in a variety of media and many guises, from studies of individual dancers rehearsing [cat. 12] or resting, as shown here [see also cat. 17], to large-scale compositions of dancers practising in the studio [cat. 16] or performing on stage. Such works were executed in graphite, chalk, ink, pastel or oil, or even three-dimensionally as in *La Danseuse de quatorze ans* (1879–81) and the sequence of ballerinas made in wax over the last twenty-five years of the artist's life.

12 Dancer Standing

Danseuse debout; c. 1880
ink heightened with white chalk on paper,
63.5 x 48.5 cm
signed lower left
L. 401
Private Collection

Unlike Degas's studies of ballet dancers made in the 1870s [see cat. 11] which he recycled over the years, the studies made in the succeeding decade appear to have been executed with a single, specific composition in mind. Generally, these studies were made on a monumental scale, before being reduced for inclusion in a larger work. The present work has the feel of a preliminary study: both the position of the upraised arm and the hemline of the tutu have been shifted. However, the sense of the figure being caught in strong stage light from below is conveyed by the highlighting of upper torso, breast, chin and right eye, and the presence of deep shadow to the left of the dancer's head.

13 Woman at her Toilette

Femme à sa toilette; 1885–90
pastel on paper, 41 x 31.5 cm
signed lower left
L. 1286
Private Collection

During the mid-1880s Degas shifted
the course of his art. He abandoned
the more complex, multi-figure compositions of the previous fifteen years
in favour of more simplified, non-
narrative compositions, dominated by
a single figure set in a shallow space.
These classicising tendencies are best
demonstrated in his sequence of large
pastels of nudes usually engaged in
some aspect of bathing in which the
line describing the figure becomes the
basis over which low-keyed pastel
colour is then placed. Degas's commitment to the importance of line was
stressed in a comment made to the
artist Walter Sickert in 1885: 'They
[Monet, Pissarro, Renoir] are all
exploiting the possibilities of colour.
And I am always begging them to
exploit the possibilities of drawing.
It is the richer field'.

cat. 14

14 Woman at her Toilette

Femme à sa toilette; c.1892
pastel on paper mounted on card, 56 x 65 cm
signed lower left
L.1126
Rudolf Staechelin Family Foundation

During the 1890s, Degas gave colour a more prominent role in his pastels once again. Yet, as Richard Kendell has pointed out, however brilliant colouristically their surfaces might be, as in the pastel shown here, the forms are described tonally as a substructure over which the colour is then laid. This accounts for the continued integrity of the form of the nude in this pastel, despite the initial eradication of her volume through the downward sweep of pastel strokes uniting background and nude figure into what appears to be a single plane. The addition of strips of paper on the left and at the top of the sheet demonstrates Degas's characteristic creative method: starting from the initial sheet he pushes the composition out towards the edges, providing himself with supplementary areas for the resolution of specific facets of the composition such as the jug on the left and space above the upraised arm.

15 The Bath, Woman Seen from Behind

Le Bain, femme vue de dos; c.1895
oil on canvas, 65 x 81 cm
L.1104
Private Collection

This painting of a nude who has just got out of her bath belongs to a remarkable group of oil paintings of nudes in movement or lying down, often in awkward or contorted poses. In this work, the difficulty in reading the image is reinforced by the fact that the gesture of the woman's arm across her thigh has lost its initial meaning, namely drying herself with a towel. This was present in a preliminary drawing but has been eliminated from the finished work. Equally remarkable in these works is the technique. Here Degas used oil paint with a new freedom, working across the layers of underpainting and applying the upper layers with a brush and with his hands. This is especially clear in this work where the dense, stippled surface seems to have been achieved almost exclusively through pigment applied with the artist's fingers.

cat. 15

16 At the Theatre: Dancers in the Wings

Scène de théâtre: danseuses au foyer; c. 1895–8
oil on canvas, 39 x 87 cm
signed lower left
L. 1394
Private Collection

Degas made frieze-like compositions of
dancers (c. 40 x c. 90 cm) from the late 1870s
to the close of the 1890s. The one shown here
is closely related to a work, *The Ballet Rehearsal*
(Yale University Art Gallery, New Haven;
L. 1107), of around 1890, which is itself related
to a contemporaneous work, *In the Rehearsal
Room* (National Gallery of Art, Washington
DC; L. 941). In all three works the figures are
arranged in a frieze in two distinct groups:
on the right, close up to the picture plane,
dancers are resting or arranging their ballet
shoes; on the left, set well into the depth of
the space, dancers practise at the bar. The
number of dancers in each work varies, but
all three incorporate some of the same poses:
the dancers on the extreme right and left of
the right-hand group in the work shown here
appeared in the Yale painting, although the
number of dancers on the left has been
reduced from four to two. This work and
that at Yale physically isolate the two groups
through the insertion of a strong vertical line
placed left of centre. While this cannot be
clearly read in the work exhibited here, the
Yale picture indicates that it is a metal pillar
supporting a ceiling above the upper edge of
the canvas. Despite the obvious dependence
on many elements found in these two earlier
friezes, the technique of dark outline and
somewhat smudged colour of the later work
relates it more closely to another frieze composition of similar dimensions executed
c. 1898 (*The Rehearsal Room*, E. G. Bührle Foundation, Zurich; L. 996).

17 Dancers Resting

Danseuses au repos; c. 1900
pastel on paper, laid down on cardboard,
83 x 107 cm
L. 1256
Private Collection

Although Lemoisne placed this work in a group of seven pastels of identical dimensions showing two dancers on a bench and dated them to *c.* 1896, Jean Sutherland Boggs (*Degas*, 1988–9, cat. no. 377) has suggested it dates from some four years later. The dancers' poses suggest weariness, and the tonality casts a note of melancholy over the scene. The work is an authoritative statement of Degas's later pastel technique. The figures are placed against what appears to be an exuberantly abstract backcloth or stage curtain, the composition united by the strong vertical strokes of orange pastel which break across and eradicate

divisions between legs and tutu, figure and backdrop. Such treatment eliminates all depth and emphasises the surface of the paper. Yet, as in his pastel studies of nudes of the previous decade [see cat. 14], a dialogue between the decorative qualities of the two-dimensional surface and the descriptive qualities of three-dimensional space is established through the modelled forms of the dancers and the gentle diagonal recession which permits us to read the left-hand dancer as existing in a space slightly behind her fellow ballerina on the right.

cat. 18

18 Dancer

Danseuse; c. 1895–1900
pastel on paper, 54.5 x 45 cm
signed lower right and upper left
L. 1350
Private Collection

The bold black outline of the dancer, accentuated
by the strong vertical marks of the warm toned pastel
behind, associate this figure with a group of studies
of dancers made around 1898 and with studies of
nudes made *c.* 1900 [see cat. 19]. In all these works large
areas of the paper are left unmarked. These serve to
represent intense light, from which Degas works away
towards shadow through the increasingly dense application of the black chalk or pastel.

19 After the Bath:
Woman Drying Herself

Après le bain: baigneuse s'essuyant; c. 1900
charcoal and pastel on three pieces of tracing paper, 68 x 36 cm
signed lower left
L. 1383
Private Collection

In the opening year of the 20th century Degas made
a group of studies of bathers in energetic poses that
evolved out of the awkward and contorted bathers of
the 1890s [see cat. 15]. In most cases these show a nude
woman sitting on the side of a tub drying her legs.
This particular pose is derived from a pastel of a bather
drying herself made *c.* 1886 (The Dayton Art Institute;
L. 917), but the format has been changed from horizontal to vertical, and the setting is restricted to the edge
of the tub, a hint of a red slipper, an indication of a red
curtain and a sketchily painted towel. As in Degas's
studies of ballet dancers of the same period [see cat. 18],
the modelling of the figure is essentially tonal,
unmarked areas of paper acting as highlights, and
shadows indicated by varying levels of hatching in
charcoal and black pastel. Only along the spine of the
nude is the drawing line permitted a degree of decorative, rather than descriptive, licence.

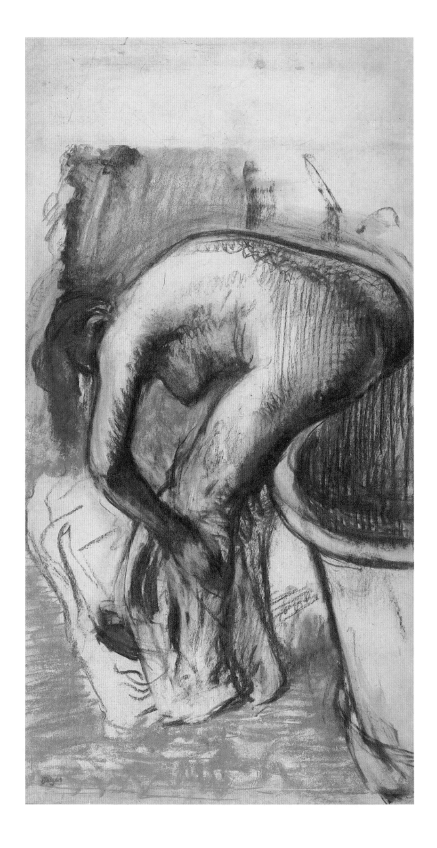

20 Self-Portrait

Autoportrait; after 1900
pastel on paper mounted on canvas, 47.5 x 32.5 cm
atelier stamp lower left
Fondation Rau pour le Tiers-Monde, Zurich

Degas made many self-portraits throughout his life.
This one, almost certainly executed in the studio,
captures both the self-knowledge of an older man
and the searching gaze of the artist whose eyesight
is already failing.

PAUL GAUGUIN

PARIS, 8 June 1848 – MARQUESAS ISLANDS, 8 May 1903

Gauguin spent his childhood in Peru (1849–55). From 1865 to 1871 he worked as a sailor; in the latter year he became employed on the Paris Stock Exchange. He started to paint around 1873, and from 1883, when he lost his job in the financial collapse, devoted himself solely to painting. Through his guardian, Gustave Arosa, he came to know the work of the Impressionists: he bought their work, befriended them and benefited from instruction from Pissarro after 1879 and from Cézanne in 1881; from 1879 he exhibited with them. Wishing to distance himself from naturalism, he studied Japanese and primitive art and sought out cultures untouched by Western civilisation. He visited Brittany, still a remote part of France, in 1886, returning in 1888 and settling there in 1889–91, becoming the 'leader' of the School of Pont-Aven. In 1887 he visited Martinique; its exoticism and intense colours confirmed his desire to escape permanently to the Tropics. In 1891 he travelled to Tahiti, returning to France between 1894 and 1895, but settling there permanently from 1895 to 1901, after which he moved to the Marquesas Islands, where he died. The first retrospective exhibition of his work was held at the Salon d'Automne in Paris in 1906.

The first work by Gauguin to enter a Swiss collection was probably a still-life, *Nature morte au plateau de fruits et citrons* (1890; W. 401), purchased by Sidney and Jenny Brown from Dr Georges Viau in 1909, one year after they bought a challenging still-life by Cézanne, *Nature morte: pêches et carafe sur une nappe*. Evidently the Gauguin was deemed to be of sufficient importance to be included in Carl Montag's selection of Impressionist and Post-Impressionist masterpieces from Swiss private collections shown in the Grosse Ausstellung held at Stuttgart in 1913, in the exhibition of French modern masters shown in Zurich in 1917, and in the Kunsthalle Basel in 1928, the only important monographic show of Gauguin's work to be shown in Switzerland before 1939. The pioneer collectors seem to have favoured Gauguin's works predating his first visit to Tahiti in 1891. Thus, a distinguished Winterthur collector acquired a still-life of 1880; Georg Reinhart acquired a still-life from Galerie Druet, Paris, on 2 May 1912; and his brother Oskar owned a landscape painted during the artist's sojourn in Rouen (*Les Toits bleus*, 1884; W. 100).

Within this context of early Swiss taste, Rudolf Staechelin's purchase of the monumental *Nafea* (1892), made during the artist's first trip to Tahiti, from Galerie Moos, Geneva, on 27 June 1917, is exceptional. To be sure, four, or possibly five Tahitian works had been included in the exhibition of nine paintings and ten lithographs mounted by Wolfensberger in his Galerie Wolfsberg, Zurich, in April 1912. The works for this exhibition had been supplied by Ambroise Vollard and their loan negotiated through the intercession of Carl Montag. A description of the exhibition was given by the English civil servant and collector Michael Sadler, but no record survives as to whether any works were sold from the show to Swiss collectors. Enthusiasm for Gauguin's exotic subjects seems to have waned, although in 1928 the Kupferstichkabinett, Basel, bought a pastel on paper of 1892, *Words of the Devil*, and Baron von Hirsch presented *Ta Matete* (*Le Marché*; W. 476) to the Kunstmuseum Basel in 1941. It was only after World War II that a taste for Gauguin's later works was firmly established. Certain collectors continued to favour his Brittany paintings of 1886 and 1888–91, but others, such as E. G. Bührle, particularly concentrated on his work dating from after 1891, and this taste was reinforced by the influx of foreign collectors into Switzerland.

21 Still-Life: Flowers for a Bouquet

Nature morte: pour faire un bouquet; 1880
oil on canvas, 56 x 66.5 cm
signed and dated lower right: 1880
W. 49
Private Collection

This work was painted while Gauguin was still employed at the Stock Exchange of Paris. He had already staked his claim to be taken seriously as a painter when he had participated in the Impressionist exhibitions of 1879 and of 1880, the year in which this still-life was painted.

The odd juxtaposition of the bouquet of flowers against a boldly decorated chair, and the ambiguous treatment of space, parallel concerns found in contemporary works, for example *Flowers: Still-Life (The Painter's Home, Rue Carcel)* (1881; W. 50). Here a bouquet of flowers stands on a table which, together with a chair set at an angle, creates a dramatic diagonal across the composition. While the spatial eccentricities of both these still-lifes may owe much to Degas's radical treatment of space, the feathery brushwork shows the influence of Pissarro, with whom Gauguin had worked the previous summer at Pontoise.

22 Village Street

Rue de village; 1884
oil on canvas, 56 x 46.5 cm
signed and dated lower left: 84
W. 126
Private Collection

The Paris Stock Market collapsed in 1882, depriving
Gauguin of a source of regular income. While release
from full-time employment allowed him to devote
himself almost exclusively to painting, the need to
support his family drove him to make economies. In
January 1884 he settled his family in cheaper accom-
modation in Rouen, and they remained in the city
until they left for Copenhagen in the summer;
Gauguin following them there in November.

This view of a village street was made in the
environs of Rouen. At this stage in his artistic development Gauguin was still open to the influence of
Pissarro, with whom he had stayed in Rouen the
previous November; he was aware of the volumetric
analysis of landscape pursued by Pissarro and
Cézanne in the previous decade, which was brought
to maturity by Cézanne after 1880 [see cat. 5, 6].

23 Winter Landscape, Copenhagen

Paysage d'hiver à Copenhague; 1885
oil on canvas, 46.5 x 32 cm
signed and dated lower left: 85
W. 143
Private Collection, Zurich

Gauguin joined his family in Copenhagen, the home
town of his wife, Mette, in November 1884. He was
to remain there until his return to Paris in June 1885.
During this six-month stay, he exhibited work at the
Society of the Friends of Art in May 1885 and wrote
his first important theoretical text, *Notes synthétiques*.
This view of a back garden in winter retains the
muted palette of his earlier landscapes; it predates
his more radical treatment of landscape made in
Normandy during the summer of 1885; in these,
intense reds and oranges punctuate the luxuriant
greens of summer growth.

24 Girls with Dogs (Sewing)

Filles aux chiens (La couseuse); 1889
oil on canvas, 73 x 92 cm
W. 358
Private Collection

Gauguin had moved to Brittany in February 1888, after his return from Martinique. It was his second visit to the province, and he chose to stay once again at the picturesque village of Pont-Aven, situated on the River Aven on the south coast. He was to remain there until he moved along the coast to Le Pouldu in October 1889 [see cat. 25].

The lush vegetation of this picture suggests that it was made at Pont-Aven during the summer of 1889. It therefore post-dates two important events in Gauguin's professional career: the

manifesto exhibition, Exposition de peintures du groupe impressionniste et synthétique, organised in June 1889 by Gauguin and two fellow artists, Emile Bernard and Emile Schuffenecker, at the Café Volpini on the Champ de Mars in Paris; and the invitation to show at the Brussels avant-garde exhibition mounted by Les XX in February 1889. These two exhibitions allowed Gauguin to proclaim his new, non-naturalist style of art. Described as 'peinture synthétique' and 'pictorial symbolism', this new style of painting involved a distancing from both obvious narrative and realistic transcription of the external world in order to reveal ideas or profound emotions. This was achieved through the simplification of form through bold outline and flat colour infill, and the elimination of traditional

modes of recession. These principles have been applied to the painting shown here with the bold outline circumscribing the two figures, the application of unmodulated colour in rigorously vertical brushstrokes and the use of a high horizon line.

The decision to show the two girls in contemporary dress rather than in Breton costume is unusual in Gauguin's work of this period. It may reflect his response to the hierarchic character of the figures in contemporary dress in Seurat's monumental painting, *Dimanche après-midi à la Grande Jatte* (1884, 1886–7; Art Institute of Chicago) which had already been incorporated into a major Breton subject painting the previous summer by Gauguin's younger colleague and fellow symbolist, Emile Bernard (see *Breton Women in a Meadow*, 1888, Private Collection).

25 The Flute Player on the Cliff

Le Joueur du flageolet sur la falaise; 1889
oil on canvas, 73 x 92 cm
signed and dated lower right: 89
W. 361
Private Collection

This painting almost certainly shows the rocky coastline above the Breton village of Le Pouldu to which Gauguin moved from Pont-Aven in October 1889.

The precipitous viewpoint, looking down on the figure, cliffs and beach, echoes similar vertiginous spatial formats found, for example, in *Seascape with Cow on the Edge of a Cliff* (1888, Musée des Arts Décoratifs, Paris; W. 282) and *Breton Girls by the Sea* (1889, The National Museum of Western Art, Tokyo; W. 340). The sweep of the beach, treated as a decorative surface, is also found in *Beach at Le Pouldu* (1889, Private Collection; W. 362). In all these works, Gauguin enclosed each element in a clear, dark outline, and exaggerated the colours to the extent that they no longer read as direct transcriptions from the external world. He also eliminated the sky from the compositions, thereby flattening out the representation of spatial recession. Painted after his trip to Martinique and the creation of his most uncompromisingly radical painting to date, *The Vision after the Sermon: Jacob Wrestling with the Angel* (1888, National Gallery of Scotland, Edinburgh; W. 245), the emphasis on outline with flat colour infill, the absence of space and the extensive application of vertical brushstrokes across the entire surface of the canvas reinforce its decorative qualities. The simplification of forms indicates that his primary intention was not the naturalistic description of the external world but rather the communication of an idea, in this case the primitive nature of Brittany. In this respect, it represents Gauguin's reaction to the naturalism of Impressionism which came to be known as 'Pictorial Symbolism'.

26 NAFEA FAA-IPOIPO: When will you Marry?

NAFEA FAA-IPOIPO: Quand te maries-tu?; 1892
oil on canvas, 101.5 x 77.5 cm
signed and dated lower left: 92
W. 454
Rudolf Staechelin Family Foundation
(on loan to the Kunstmuseum Basel)

During both his stays in Tahiti (1891–3; 1895–1901), Gauguin made a number of compositions dominated by one or two monumental figures. Most of these bear titles intended to be understood as Tahitian, some of which were provided with translations, as is the case of the painting shown here. The meaning is probably intentionally enigmatic: which of the two girls is being questioned, and by whom? It has been suggested that the girl crouching in the foreground with a flower tucked behind her ear may be the object of such an inquiry.

The painting almost certainly dates from the latter months of 1892: the 'pua' flower that adorns the crouching girl blossoms in December and there is a sketch of the two girls on the back of a sheet of studies for *Aha oe feii? (What! Are you Jealous?)* (1892, Pushkin Museum of Fine Art, Moscow; W. 461), a painting almost certainly completed in the autumn of 1892.

The crouching figure was probably derived from the second figure on the right in Eugène Delacroix's *Femmes d'Alger* (1834, Musée du Louvre, Paris). Gauguin had a lifelong admiration for Delacroix; he also viewed his own journeys to Tahiti as a parallel to the older painter's search for the exotic and the noble primitive in North Africa in 1830.

This painting was sent back to Paris in 1893 for exhibition at Durand-Ruel's gallery. Gauguin obviously valued it highly, for he assigned it and one other work the highest price in that exhibition. It may also have been included in his posthumous retrospective exhibition held in the Salon d'Automne, Paris, in 1906.

27 Self-Portrait

Portrait de l'artiste; c. 1903
oil on canvas, 32 x 26 cm
atelier stamp lower left
W. 633
Private Collection

Gauguin moved from Tahiti to the Marquesas Islands in September 1901. Sick, poor and at odds with the local European community, this was his last self-portrait painted before his death on 8 May 1903.

EDOUARD MANET

PARIS, 23 January 1832 – PARIS, 30 April 1883

Manet was born into comfortable circumstances in Paris. He entered the atelier of Thomas Couture in 1849 but derived equally important lessons from copying Italian and Spanish Old Masters both in the Louvre and abroad, notably in Italy, Holland and Germany. His admiration for the works of Velázquez, Murillo and Zurbarán led him to paint subjects inspired by Spain in the early 1860s and to visit that country in 1865. After 1859, his subject-matter was almost exclusively derived from modern urban life. Despite frequent rejection, he regularly submitted these paintings to the Salon. The controversial nature of both subject-matter and technique, which led to his inclusion in the Salon des Refusés in 1863, established Manet as the focus of a younger generation of naturalist writers and artists including the Impressionists who gathered at the Café Guerbois. He won notoriety with his paintings of *Déjeuner sur l'herbe* (1862), *Olympia* (1863) and *Un Bar aux Folies-Bergère* (1881–2). Despite being encouraged by Monet to sketch out of doors in the early 1870s, Manet never exhibited at the Impressionist exhibitions. Towards the end of his life he concentrated increasingly on portraits of women, in both oil and pastel, still-lifes and views of suburban gardens.

Arthur and Hedy Hahnloser acquired the sketch for Monet's *L'Amazone* (Villa Flora Stiftung, Winterthur) which they subsequently lent to the exhibition, Meisterwerke aus Privatsammlungen, Winterthur, in 1922. Some time before 1931, Arthur Hahnloser's brother, Emil, acquired from Vollard Manet's *Portrait de Berthe Morisot au chapeau de deuil* (1874, Private Collection, Zurich; RW. 228). Given the character of both of these collections, the acquisitions were unusual. More understandable was the purchase of four Manets, two from Fritz Nathan, which Oskar Reinhart made for his collection at his house, Am Römerholz, after 1919. It would appear that Manet's capacity to stand as 'the painter of modern life' and also to work in the tradition marked out by Velázquez, Frans Hals and Delacroix gave to him a unique position in the evolution of European art, one which suited Reinhart's collection. A similar sentiment seems to have informed Rudolf Staechelin's purchase of a *Tête de femme* (1870; RW. 156) in 1917. Sidney and Jenny Brown, however, never bought a work by Manet.

Works by Manet figure more prominently in the collections of later generations. Jacques Koerfer, after he had moved from Hamburg to Bern, purchased the more finished version of *L'Amazone* (RW. 271). E. G. Bührle acquired his first Manet, *Rue Mosnier avec drapeaux* (1878) from Siegfried Rosengart, Lucerne, in 1937. He subsequently bought a number of works by the artist either from Fritz Nathan or through galleries in Paris and New York. More recently, another variant of the view of the Rue Mosnier, *La rue Mosnier aux paveurs* (1878; RW. 272), was bought by a private corporation and is now in a collection in the canton of Ticino.

28 The Port of Calais

Le Port de Calais; 1871
oil on canvas, 81.5 x 100.7 cm
W. 174
Private Collection

After the harrowing experiences of the Siege of Paris and the Commune, in August 1871 Manet retreated with his family to Boulogne-sur-Mer. While there he made an excursion up the coast to Calais, which produced the painting shown here. Manet had already stayed in Boulogne-sur-Mer, possibly in 1868 and certainly in 1869. On those visits he painted views of the port, not conventional port scenes in the manner of Claude-Joseph Vernet's late 18th-century paintings of the ports of France, but scenes with all the bustle of contemporary life (*The Departure of the Folkestone Ferry*, 1869, Philadelphia Museum of Fine Arts; RW. 147), under moonlight (*Moonlight over Boulogne Harbour*, 1869, Musée d'Orsay, Paris; RW. 143), or with eccentric viewpoints, as in *The Pier at Boulogne* (1869, Private Collec-

tion; RW. 145). In 1871 he had already painted a view of another port, Bordeaux, where he had gone to join his family in February (*The Port of Bordeaux*, Private Collection; RW. 164). The work shown here retains the simplification of forms, created by the use of broad areas of colour and the lack of modulating zones between the juxtapositions of light and shade, characteristic of many of Manet's marine paintings from 1864 onwards.

CLAUDE MONET

PARIS, 14 November 1840 – GIVERNY, 5 December 1926

The son of a Parisian shop-keeper who moved to Le Havre when Monet was five, he returned to Paris in 1869 and studied at the Académie Suisse where he met Pissarro. After military service in Algeria he returned to Le Havre, where he met Boudin and Jongkind, who encouraged his efforts at painting landscapes out of doors. Back in Paris in 1863, he met the future Impressionists Bazille, Renoir and Sisley at Gleyre's studio. Together they painted in the Forest of Fontainebleau. Influenced by Manet's paintings of contemporary life and having studied Delacroix's use of complementary colours, Monet and Renoir evolved the Impressionist technique in the autumn of 1869 when they were working at La Grenouillère on the River Seine. In an attempt to convey the fleeting effects of nature, pure colour was applied in rapid, comma-like brushstrokes onto a lightly primed canvas. Monet was a founder of the Impressionist exhibitions in 1874, where he showed *Impression, Sunrise* (1873, Musée Marmottan, Paris) that gave its name to the Impressionist movement. Towards the end of the 1870s he confronted the problem of Impressionism: that the technique was unable to imbue an image of the external world with a sense of permanence. In the 1880s he travelled to the French and Italian Rivieras, employing a more brilliant palette, and adopting the compositional techniques of Japanese prints. After settling in a house in Giverny in 1883 he began work on the series of paintings that included the *Poplars* (1892), the *Haystacks* (1890–1), and the façade of *Rouen Cathedral* (1892–4); these culminated in the sequence of vast canvases recording the water-lily pond in his garden.

Monet does not seem to have enjoyed the same popularity with early collectors in Switzerland as did his fellow Impressionists Sisley and Pissarro. Whereas Josef Müller apparently had admired Pissarro at an exhibition in Zurich in 1908, and Sidney and Jenny Brown purchased a work by that artist in 1909 (*La Cueillette des pois à Eragny*, 1893; PV.857), Müller never bought a work by Monet, and only one was acquired by the Browns, *La Débâcle de la Seine* (1893; W.1344), bought from Dr Georges Viau in April 1910, together with another eight major works. It was one of two paintings by Monet which Carl Montag recommended to the Browns in a letter dated 14 March 1910. The other work, a *Falaise à Etretat* of 1883, was not purchased, perhaps due to the fact that both its composition and technique were more radical than the harmonious painting of 1893. Arthur and Hedy Hahnloser had also purchased a Monet before 1920, but when their collection was exhibited at the Kunstmuseum Lucerne in 1940, only one of his works was included, in contrast to twenty-seven oils by Bonnard, five by Cézanne, thirteen by Van Gogh and seventeen by Renoir.

Despite a joint exhibition of the work of Monet and Jongkind held at the Galerie Paul Vallotton in Lausanne in 1917, no significant retrospective of Monet's work was held in Switzerland before 1939. While Paul Durand-Ruel, who acted as Monet's chief commercial dealer in Paris, was a regular source of new acquisitions for many of the Swiss collectors, his championship of Monet's work does not seem to have been reflected in their collections. Rudolf Staechelin acquired the coastal cliff scene, *Temps calme, Fécamp* (1881; W.650), from Kunstsalon Ludwig Schames, Frankfurt, in 1918, and E. G. Bührle bought his first Monet in 1924. Bührle subsequently bought other works during the 1940s from, among others, Fritz Nathan.

In recent decades the taste for Monet has developed in Switzerland, in particular for his later work, as is demonstrated by the number of private collectors who lent to the 1986 Basel Kunstmuseum exhibition, Claude Monet: Nympheas.

29 Honfleur: Sailing Boats

Bateaux à Honfleur; 1866
oil on canvas, 55.5 x 46.5 cm
signed lower left
W. 75
Private Collection

Monet had spent his childhood in Le Havre.
From the mid-1850s, in his formative years as
a painter, and throughout the following four
decades, he regularly visited the Channel coast,
working at the picturesque fishing port of
Honfleur or the seaside resorts of Ste Adresse,
Trouville and Etretat, or recording the more
desolate coastline near Fécamp and Dieppe
[see cat. 33, 38, 39].

This painting of fishing boats at Honfleur
is a preliminary study for a large finished work,
The Port of Honfleur (W. 77). Although painted in
front of the motif, it does not yet reveal an
understanding of how forms are broken up
and dispersed by light in the true Impressionist
manner. Rather, its flatly laid-in paint, muted
palette and sharp contrasts of light and shadow
recall the handling of similar subjects by Manet
[see cat. 28] and Courbet. In particular, the representation of the water, with its dense textures
and the generally unbroken reflections of the
boats, gives it a thick, static character. The
problem of indicating reflections in water with
both form and movement was addressed by
Monet during the late 1860s, most notably in his
scenes made at La Grenouillère in the autumn
of 1869 (*La Grenouillère*, 1869, The Metropolitan
Museum of Art, New York, W. 134; *Les Bains
de la Grenouillère*, 1869, National Gallery,
London, W. 135).

30 Old Rue de la Chaussée, Argenteuil

L'Ancienne rue de la Chaussée, Argenteuil;
1872
oil on canvas, 55 x 73 cm
signed lower right
W. 239
Private Collection

On his return from Holland in November 1871, Monet moved to Argenteuil, a town situated on the River Seine to the north-west of Paris, which had become a centre for boating during the second half of the 19th century. He was to remain there until his move to Vétheuil in 1878.

During his six-year residence, Monet recorded many different aspects of the town: the river as the place for leisure boating and professional regattas, and as the site of growing industrialisation; the road and newly reconstructed rail bridges that spanned the river from Petit Gennevilliers to Argenteuil, and the town itself. This painting shows an older quarter of Argenteuil. Instead of using short, comma-like brushstrokes, which became Monet's means of rapidly transcribing nature, here the paint is laid in broadly, and the sharp contrast of light and shade and the overall blond tonality suggest that he was still seeking to capture luminosity in a landscape through *peinture claire*. In this respect this painting has much in common with works by Sisley and Pissarro dating from the same year.

31 Sailing Boat at Argenteuil

Le Voilier à Argenteuil; c. 1872
oil on canvas, 65 x 61 cm
signed lower right
W. 197
Private Collection

The presence of the sailing boat in the middle distance of this painting, set against a view of Argenteuil, recalls that the town had become one of the centres for yachting around 1850. The town was linked to Paris by the railway in 1851; the previous year it had sponsored a sailing regatta to persuade the Parisians of the exceptional facilities offered by this stretch of the River Seine, and in 1858 it had succeeded in luring the prestigious sailing club, Le Cercle des Voiliers, to relocate its headquarters in the town.

The rapid laying-in of the paint, using short, comma-like brushstrokes, captures the fresh, breezy weather conditions. A comparison with the flatter, more broadly handled paint found both in Monet's *Old Rue de la Chaussée, Argenteuil* [cat. 30] and in a work by Sisley of almost the same view as the one shown here (*Boats on the Seine at Argenteuil*, 1872, Private Collection; D. 122) shows how successfully Monet had developed a method for the visual notation of changing light across a landscape during his early years at Argenteuil.

32 The Kamperhoofd, Amsterdam

Vue du Kamperhoofd à Amsterdam; ?1873
oil on canvas, 61 x 101.5 cm
signed lower left
W. 303
Fondation Rau pour le Tiers-Monde, Zurich

Monet and his wife, Camille, arrived in Holland from London early in June 1871. They passed the summer in Zaandam, moving to Amsterdam in early October. Monet's paintings of Amsterdam, of which at least twelve survive, are undated but seem stylistically to belong to 1873 or 1874. Although there is no documentary evidence, it has been assumed that Monet may have made at least two very brief visits to the city after 1871.

The present view was painted from the Oosterdijk looking west. The views he chose to paint in Amsterdam are mostly located in groups close to each other; the present painting is related to another work, *The Kamperhoofd and the Oude Waal* (1871, Private Collection; W. 304) which was made further east along the Kamperhoofd.

Monet has used the same peremptory brushwork that is found in many of the other Amsterdam paint-

ings: paint is applied in short, rapid strokes, or *taches*, over a coloured priming which is often left uncovered and thus acts as part of the final colour scheme. The format of the canvas of this painting is exceptional for the Amsterdam group, being a size which Monet also used in Argenteuil in 1873 and at Le Havre in January 1874.

Claude Monet 82

33 Low Tide at Pourville

Marée basse à Pourville; 1882
oil on canvas, 58 x 100 cm
signed and dated lower left: 82
W. 776
Private Collection

After working almost exclusively in the Seine Basin during the 1870s [see cat. 30, 31], Monet began to travel more extensively after 1880. Like his fellow Impressionists [see cat. 47, 60], he had become increasingly concerned about the ability of Impressionism to provide anything other than an ephemeral record of nature. While Renoir turned to a form of classicism derived from the Antique and the High Renaissance [see cat. 60], and Pissarro adopted the more rigorous method of Neo-Impressionism [see cat. 47, 48], Monet sought out new subject-matter, often recorded under the more extreme lighting effects found in the South of France and on the Normandy coast, and turned again to Japanese prints as a source of formal solutions.

Monet had first visited the Normandy coast around Dieppe in 1881, working at Varengeville and Pourville. While this view of the chalk cliffs near Varengeville has none of the colouristic experimenta-

tion found in his views of the church at Varengeville made during the same visit, nor the innovatory compositions of his views along the cliffs at Fécamp of the previous year, the self-conscious division of the composition along the horizon into two equal parts, making the lower half the mirror image of sky and cliff which constitute the upper half, introduces an element of stability into a view which records a windy day and broken light cast on the scene through the scudding clouds in the sky. This search for stability in his landscapes was also explored by Monet in his views of the church at Vétheuil across the River Seine, in the winter scenes on the Seine at Lavacourt, and ultimately in the series paintings on which he embarked in 1890 [see cat. 37, 38, 39].

34 Val de Falaise (Giverny): Winter

Val de Falaise en hiver; 1885
oil on canvas, 65.4 x 80.5 cm
signed and dated lower left: 85
W. 976
Private Collection

The bank and wooden barrier cutting across the lower part of this composition, the screen of pollarded trees and the high horizon line all conspire to make this painting spatially awkward. It has much in common with Monet's experiments in radical spatial relationships in his works of the early 1880s, for example, views of the cliffs at Fécamp of 1881 and the disconnected foreground and background in his paintings of the church at Varengeville.

cat. 35

35 Haystacks at Giverny

Les Meules à Giverny; 1885
oil on canvas, 65 x 81 cm
signed and dated lower left: 85
W. 993
Private Collection

Monet moved to Giverny in 1883; he was to live there until his death in 1926, deriving the vast majority of his motifs from the surrounding countryside or from his own garden [see cat. 34]. This painting combines motifs that Monet was subsequently to study in isolation: the four informally presented figures on the left are pursued further in *Five Figures in a Field* (1888, Art Institute of Chicago); the line of poplar trees occurs first as a dense screen in *Poplars at Giverny* (1887, Private Collection, Boston; W. 1155), and later as serpentine patterns under different light and weather conditions in the series of *Poplars on the River Epte* of 1891. The haystacks were the precursors of the grainstacks, observed either alone or in pairs under snow or frost, morning or evening light, in the first fully fledged series paintings made by Monet in 1890–1.

The handling of the paint, the range of colour and the formal organisation of the composition illustrate the various solutions devised by Monet by the mid-1880s to resolve problems inherent in Impressionism at the end of the previous decade. The composition, punctuated by the three lumpy haystacks, has been arranged in three parallel bands: field in the fore-ground, line of poplars in the middle ground, and sky with, on the right, a hint of hills in the background. Monet adopted different brushwork for each band to underline their integrity: loose, random strokes for the field; tighter, more systematic strokes for the poplars; and thin, broad strokes for the sky. The greater intensity of colours, even in areas of shadow, does not eliminate their traditional descriptive function, but does indicate Monet's increasing concern to give them another role. In this case, by emphasising zones of dominant colour, Monet superimposed a two-dimensional pattern upon the three-dimensional scene.

36 Belle-Ile (Storm)

Belle-Ile (orage); 1886
oil on canvas, 60 x 73 cm
signed lower right
W. 1117
Private Collection

Apart from brief, but unrecorded, visits to Amsterdam, Monet worked mostly in the Seine Valley in the 1870s. From the early 1880s he started to travel further afield, to the Normandy coast near Dieppe [see cat. 33], the South of France and Brittany. It was almost certainly Renoir and Octave Mirbeau who encouraged the artist to explore Brittany, but it was the descriptions given in a guide-book which led him to the rocky Breton island of Belle-Ile, off the south coast. On arriving in September 1886 he initially recorded the rocky cliffs and promontories of the island under calm, sunlit conditions. However, the storms which hit the island in October encouraged him to stay to capture the drama of the wind-lashed waves as they thundered in from the Atlantic. Although many of the paintings Monet made during September appear to have been finished in his studio after he left the coast of Brittany in November 1886, the paintings that record the storm effects are so rapidly executed and have so little evidence of major compositional adjustments that they may well have been painted on the spot. The painting shown here retains traces of the initial outline rapidly put in with a thin brush, and is executed in swirling, gestural brushstrokes which capture with immediacy the extreme weather conditions.

37 Rouen Cathedral. Façade and Tour d'Albane (Morning Effect)

La Cathédrale de Rouen. Le Portail et la Tour d'Albane:
le matin; 1892–4
oil on canvas, 106.7 x 73.7 cm
signed and dated lower left: 94
W. 1347
Beyeler Collection, Basel

Despite a preliminary group of paintings made in 1889 of the Grande and Petite Creuse, it was with his group of grainstacks made in 1890–1 that Monet embarked upon his sequence of ten groups of paintings, each conceived as a series, which were to dominate his output in the 1890s. He took a single motif – a line of poplars, a view on the River Seine, the Japanese bridge in his garden or the façade of Rouen Cathedral – and recorded it under changing light and weather conditions.

Monet started his series of the west façade of Rouen Cathedral in early spring 1892. He was to return to the motif again in 1893. Over the years 1892–4 he painted thirty canvases, all but two showing the façade from three slightly different angles; the remaining two focused on the Tour d'Albane alone. Twenty of these canvases were later worked up in his studio in Giverny and were exhibited to great critical acclaim at Durand-Ruel's galleries in May 1895. Monet was concerned to convey not the materiality of the elaborate Gothic stone building but rather the effect of light falling upon it, and he created a veil of tinted air between his eye and the stone façade itself.

38 Val St Nicolas, near Dieppe (Morning)

Le Val St Nicolas près de Dieppe, le matin;
1896–7
oil on canvas, 65 x 92 cm
signed lower right
W. 1433
Private Collection

Monet was drawn to the elemental grandeur of the high chalk cliffs that marked the northern coastline of Normandy and had painted them regularly between 1881 and 1886 [see cat. 33], producing some 150 works. He returned to the coast at Dieppe and Pourville between February 1896 and April 1897, painting a further fifty canvases. These fell into three groups: the beach and cliffs at Pourville, the gorge and headlands of the Petit Ailly at Varengeville [see cat. 39] and the Val St Nicolas near Dieppe, which he subsequently collectively entitled *Falaises* (Cliffs) when twenty-four of them were exhibited in 1898. Despite their different geographic locations, there is a considerable degree of tonal affinity between the three groups.

This view of the Val St Nicolas is one of the most mysterious of the group: the emerging sun has caught the morning mist in such a way that the breakwater and distant cliffs, recorded in other paintings of the same motif, have been erased. Scale and spatial relationships are implied almost exclusively through the flight of the seagulls hovering above the headland.

39 Customs Post at Varengeville

La Cabane du douanier à Varengeville; 1897
oil on canvas, 65 x 92 cm
signed, dated and dedicated lower left: à mon ami
Chéret Claude Monet 97
W. 1449
Private Collection

This view of the customs post at Varengeville, near Dieppe, shows the small hut set above the Gorge du Petit Ailly. The painting belongs to one of the three groups of paintings made on the Normandy coast between February 1896 and April 1897 which Monet collectively entitled *Falaises* (Cliffs) when he exhibited them in 1898 [see cat. 38].

Monet had already explored the cliff tops at Varengeville in 1882, making two paintings of the path leading to the customs post. In these, however, he still provided a sense of recession by allowing the horizon line to run below the cliff top. In his series of 1896–7, the horizon line established by the sea is either placed close to the top of the canvas or, as in the painting shown here, aligned with the cliff top itself. This tends to flatten out the space, thus focusing the eye on the oscillation of closely harmonised colour which activates the surface of the composition.

The painting was given by Monet to the poster designer and lithographer Jules Chéret.

40 Pergola with Roses

L'Allée de rosiers; 1920–2
oil on canvas, 89 x 100 cm
atelier stamp lower right
W. 1936
Private Collection

Monet continued to work in series from 1900 until the end of his life. Some of his motifs were drawn from foreign travel, for example the Houses of Parliament series of 1904 and the Venice series of 1908, but most were derived from the artist's garden at Giverny. Painted over more extended periods of time, they include variations on the theme of water-lilies, the Japanese bridge and the rose pergola. Work on each canvas became increasingly protracted and, despite mixed reactions from contemporary critics, it was works such as the one shown here, in which paint is laid on in expressive gestures over large areas of canvas to establish zones of colour and only secondarily to define shapes, that later came to play a formative role in the development of Abstract Expressionism in the 1940s.

CAMILLE PISSARRO

ST THOMAS (WEST INDIES), 10 July 1830 – PARIS, 13 November 1903

Pissarro travelled to Paris in 1855. Here he attended the Académie Suisse, where he met Monet, studied the works of Delacroix, Corot and Courbet and painted landscapes out of doors. During the Franco–Prussian War (1870–1) he moved to London, where he joined Monet. On his return to France in 1871 he lived at Pontoise and then settled at Eragny in 1884. While at Pontoise, he was joined by Cézanne, and for two years (1874–6) the artists shared their experience of painting in front of nature, Cézanne discovering the lighter Impressionist palette and Pissarro the elements of imposing a structure on a subject drawn directly from nature through colour and direction of brushstrokes.

An exhibitor at the 1863 Salon des Refusés, Pissarro was a leading force in the eight Impressionist exhibitions held between 1874 and 1886. Like his fellow Impressionists, however, he experienced unease with the technique at the beginning of the 1880s; he increased the scale of his figures relative to their surroundings and under the influence of Seurat he investigated the potential of Neo-Impressionism. By the end of the decade, however, following a reassessment of the work of J. M. W. Turner, he returned to a modified form of Impressionism applied to landscapes and townscapes, especially Rouen and Paris, seen at different times of day and under a variety of weather conditions.

In 1911, the Berlin dealer Paul Cassirer offered to put together an exhibition of his much sought-after Impressionist works for the Kunsthaus, Zurich. In December, thirty-five works by Monet, Renoir, Degas, Pissarro and Sisley were shown in Zurich and then transported to Basel to be shown at the Kunsthalle as the Januar-Ausstellung (Französische Impressionisten). From this exhibition, a painting, L'Hermitage, Pontoise (PV. 447), was bought by three Basel citizens, Paul and Karl Burckhardt and Hermann Meyer, and presented to the Kunstkommission of the Kunstmuseum Basel on 23 January 1913. Thus a painting by Pissarro became the first French Impressionist work to enter a Swiss public collection. That summer, Gustav Tanner, the Zurich dealer with a special relationship with Bernheim-Jeune, Paris, opened a monographic exhibition of the artist's

work at his Moderne Galerie Zurich. This exhibition had been in large measure arranged through Carl Montag in Paris, and one of Montag's clients, Sidney Brown, bought from the show a work entitled Femme écossant des pois dans un jardin (c. 1877; PV. 422).

This was not Brown's first acquisition of a painting by Pissarro. On the advice of Montag, Sidney and Jenny Brown had bought Pissarro's La Cueillette des pois à Eragny (PV. 857) from Dr Georges Viau in November 1909. Over the next seven years, they acquired a further six works, two major ones being bought in April 1910, again from Dr Viau: Boulevard Montmartre au printemps (1897; PV. 998) and Châtaigniers à Louveciennes, printemps (1870; PV. 88). While the enthusiasm for Pissarro's works among the pioneer collectors tended to mirror that for the work of Sisley, such that neither the Hahnlosers nor Georg Reinhart collected them, others showed a positive interest in his work. In the 1917 Zurich exhibition, Französische Kunst des XIX. und XX. Jahrhunderts, not only were a relatively large number of Pissarros shown (eleven works) but four of these came from private collections: no. 154 ('Ferme près de Pointoise') from an anonymous collection; no. 155 ('Val Hermé'), almost certainly lent by Hans Schuler; no. 156 ('Village'), almost certainly Landscape in the Woods at L'Hermitage (1878; PV. 444) owned by Emil Staub-Terlinden; and no. 157 ('Environs de Pontoise'), lent by Edouard Sturzenegger of St Gallen. Sturzenegger later bought from Fritz Nathan an early landscape, Au bord de la rivière, Pontoise (PV. 160), which is now in the Kunstmuseum, St Gallen. In addition, Rudolf Staechelin owned seven works by Pissarro, including La Fenaison [cat. 50], thus making him the best represented Impressionist in that collection and numerically as strong as Hodler.

Major works by Pissarro have entered Swiss private collections after 1945. Emil Georg Bührle acquired La Route de Versailles à Louveciennes (1870; PV. 96) from an American dealer in 1952, and the Fondation Rau now possesses the monumental landscape of the later 1860s, Vue de l'Hermitage [cat. 41].

41 View of the Hermitage, Côté du Jallais, Pontoise

Vue de l'Hermitage, Côté du Jallais, Pontoise;
1868
oil on canvas, 70 x 100 cm
signed lower right
PV. 57
Fondation Rau pour le Tiers-Monde, Zurich

This work belongs to a group of large-scale paintings made during Pissarro's first sojourn in Pontoise (1866–8; see also PV. 55, 56, 58, 61). All these paintings show Pissarro incorporating lessons learnt from his immediate predecessors, notably Corot, Courbet and Daubigny, in terms of composition and the application of paint. Mostly they depict houses interspersed with foliage in the middle plane integrated into carefully demarcated fore-, middle- and backgrounds which have been analysed through the imposition of a bold pattern of vigorous, heavily loaded brushstrokes. This use of colour and brushwork to impose unity upon a landscape was explored more rigorously when Pissarro worked with Cézanne around Pontoise during the following decade [see cat. 3].

42 View of Marly-le-Roi

Vue de Marly-le-Roi; 1870
oil on canvas, 47 x 71 cm
signed and dated lower right: 1870
PV. 93
Private Collection

In the late spring of 1868, Pissarro settled in the village of Louveciennes to the west of Paris between Versailles and St Germain-en-Laye. Marly-le-Roi, on the edge of the Parc de Marly, was some three kilometres north-west of Louveciennes on the road to St Germain-en-Laye. This view across the fields towards the village and church of Marly-le-Roi makes no reference to the vestigial remains of Louis XIV's spectacular sequence of follies, water basins and plantations which had once constituted the Parc de Marly. Rather it celebrates a bucolic French landscape in high summer. Five years later, Alfred Sisley was to paint almost exactly the same view cloaked in snow (Musée d'Orsay, Paris; D. 193).

43 Landscape at Louveciennes

Paysage à Louveciennes; 1870
oil on canvas, 46 x 55 cm
signed and dated lower right: 1870
PV. 98
Private Collection

Pissarro lived at 22 Route de Versailles in Louveciennes from late spring 1868 to September 1870, returning there briefly at the end of June 1871 after the collapse of the Paris Commune before moving to Pontoise in spring 1872. The house was next to the celebrated aqueduct of Marly, constructed by Louvois between 1681 and 1684 to bring water pumped from the River Seine to reservoirs on the outskirts of Louveciennes, whence it was used to supply the elaborate water works and basins of Versailles and Marly. This view almost certainly records the small farmhouse which stood close to the upper end of the aqueduct screened by trees on the left of the composition. Despite its monumentality and historical significance, the

aqueduct was only once recorded by Pissarro, and then only as a distant point in a panoramic view of Louveciennes (*Printemps à Louveciennes*, c. 1870, Tate Gallery, London; PV. 85). Sisley gave the aqueduct a central role in a compositionally far more radical work made some four years later (*L'Aqueduc de Marly*, 1874, Toledo Museum of Art; D. 133).

44 Landscape near Louveciennes: Summer

Paysage aux environs de Louveciennes en été; 1870
oil on canvas, 41 x 65 cm
signed and dated lower left: 1870
PV. 104
Private Collection

This work, dated 1870 and subtitled 'Summer', must
have been painted shortly before Pissarro and his
family fled from Louveciennes to Montfoucault, and
ultimately to London, before the advancing Prussian
armies marching on Paris. The small path on the left
appears to draw the spectator into the composition –
a device adopted from Corot and repeatedly used by
Pissarro in works made during the previous five years.
However, the central position of the tree in the foreground, disrupting any logical spatial recession, creates
an almost deliberately gauche composition, suggesting
parallels with Pissarro's more radical works of the
1870s, notably *Gelée blanche, ancienne route d'Ennery,
Pontoise* (1873, Musée d'Orsay, Paris; PV. 203).

45 The River Seine at Port-Marly

La Seine à Port-Marly; 1871
oil on canvas, 44 x 60 cm
signed and dated lower right: 1871
PV. 122
Private Collection

This view of the River Seine at Port-Marly, the small river port lying immediately below Marly-le-Roi, shows a cluster of houses in the middle distance and the promenade along the river bank shaded by an avenue of poplar trees. The painting illustrates the various functions which the River Seine served on its course from Rouen to Paris. Its commercial use is illustrated by the presence of a paddle steamer belching smoke and moving swiftly upstream ahead of a pair of more sedate barges; its more leisurely uses are implied in the elegantly clad couple who stroll along the promenade, their way punctuated by shafts of sunlight filtering through the trees, while a fisherman casts his line in the water. From the slight autumnal shades of the trees, it must be presumed that this painting was made after Pissarro's return to Louveciennes from London in late June 1871, before he moved to Pontoise the following spring.

While Pissarro recorded at least two other views of this part of the River Seine, both slightly further upstream at Bougival (PV. 95 and 125), Sisley was to work extensively at Port-Marly, creating sequences of paintings in 1872 and again in 1875.

46 The Factory on the Banks of the Oise

La Fabrique au bord de l'Oise; 1873
oil on canvas, 45 x 55 cm
signed and dated lower left: 1873
PV. 219
Private Collection, Zurich
(not exhibited)

Unlike his fellow Impressionists, who concentrated almost exclusively upon recording the more leisurely aspects of rural and suburban life, Pissarro focused on the 'working' landscape, showing various types of agrarian activity or the recent intrusion of industrial plant in the landscape. In 1868 he had produced a small group of works showing the industrial quarter of Pontoise along the Quai du Pothuis on the River Oise. Five years later he returned to the area, this time selecting the bank of the Oise opposite Pontoise at St Ouen-l'Aumône to paint a small group of factory views. Four of them record the factory of Chalon et Cie (PV. 214, 215, 217 and 218); the one shown here appears to be of a different factory. All five paintings, however, share common pictorial concerns, namely the counterpoint between the horizontality of the river and its banks and the verticality of the chimney stacks, the billowing smoke and their reflection in the water below. Pissarro was to return to a celebration of industrial landscapes in his series showing the industrialised quarters of Rouen painted between 1894 and 1897.

47 Two Peasant Women Talking

Paysannes causant; c. 1881
oil on canvas, 35 x 27 cm
signed lower left
PV. 530
Private Collection

Throughout the 1860s and '70s, Pissarro's land-scapes had normally included relatively small-scale figures that served to indicate the specific use of the land (potato gatherers, harvesters) or to act as markers of spatial recession. However, as early as 1874, in correspondence with the critic Théodore Duret, he had expressed a desire to make genre paintings of 'figures and animals in the real countryside'. Despite some initial exercises in rural genre scenes executed in the later 1870s, it was only in the subsequent decade, possibly spurred by the publication of Alfred Sensier's biography of J. F. Millet in 1881, that he shifted his attention to large-scale figures in rural or urban settings [see also cat. 48, 50]. In this painting two peasant women in dappled sunlight pause to talk beside the road. This painting was first owned by Paul Gauguin.

48 Seated Peasant Women, Talking

Paysannes assises, causant; 1881
oil on canvas, 60.4 x 73 cm
signed and dated lower right: 81
PV. 536
Private Collection

Once Pissarro had accorded a more dominant position to figures in his landscapes, he was confronted with two technical issues: the spatial relationship between figure and surrounding space, and the pictorial unity of the figure and its environment. In this painting, the precipitous, seemingly awkward placing of the two figures in relation to the steep bank initially suggests an incompetence in handling spatial relationships. Yet, such spatial eccentricity can be found in several contemporary works (*Le Repos, paysanne couchée sur l'herbe*, 1882, PV. 565; *Paysannes gardant des vaches, Pontoise*, 1882, PV. 567), and suggests that, apart from reassessing genre peasant subjects through reference to the work of J. F. Millet, Pissarro might also have been studying the work of Degas, in which similarly

ambiguous space is conveyed through the adoption of unusual viewpoints. The need to unite figures and surroundings into a whole dictated the application of a uniform handling of delicate, criss-cross brushwork to the whole painting. Such a procedure [see also cat. 47] derives from the visual experimentation undertaken by Pissarro in collaboration with Cézanne during the 1870s, where increasing uniformity of directional brushwork came both to describe the structure of a landscape and to unite apparently disparate elements within a single canvas.

49 Seated Peasant Woman with Goats

Paysanne aux chèvres; 1883–5
distemper and gouache on paper, 80.5 x 81 cm
signed and dated lower right: 1885
non-PV
Private Collection

A previously unrecorded work by Pissarro, this picture in tempera and gouache is closely related to a painting entitled *Paysanne assise et chèvre*, dated 1884 (PV. 650). The pose and position of the girl is virtually identical in both works. Whereas the composition of the oil painting is dominated by the figure of the goat girl, in the work shown here the orchard in which she is seated is extended to include a line of trees in the distance. Pissarro shared with Degas an interest in different media and their specific pictorial properties. During the 1880s he worked in gouache, pastel and distemper [see cat. 50] (see also *Le Marché à la volaille, Gisors*, 1885, PV. 1400).

50 Haymaking

La Fenaison; 1889
distemper and gouache on paper, 64.5 x 54 cm
signed and dated lower left: 1889
PV. 1442
Rudolf Staechelin Family Foundation

Peasants engaged in agrarian pursuits, for example picking apples, harvesting, gleaning or, as here, haymaking, constantly figure in Pissarro's work of the 1880s. This work relates to a group of such subjects in both pastel and oil, observed in the fields outside Gisors, the town near Eragny-sur-Epte where Pissarro came to live in April 1884. Placing the major group of figures at the centre of the composition on what appears to be slightly elevated ground focuses attention on them and allows the landscape to slip away on either side. In this respect, *Haymaking* shares a compositional device with two other works of almost the same date: *Les Glaneuses* (1889, Dreyfus Foundation, Kunstmuseum, Basel; PV. 730) and *La Cueillette des*

pommes, Eragny-sur-Epte (1888, Dallas Museum of Art; PV. 726).

Haymaking also retains some vestigial elements of divisionist technique. Pissarro had adopted the procedures of Seurat and Signac in the mid-1880s, hoping to give greater order to Impressionism by providing it with a scientific explanation of the translation of light into colour. He eventually abandoned the technique towards the end of the 1880s, arguing that it was too laborious and incapable of capturing the immediate sensation of nature, but it did enhance the range of his palette and provide him with a greater understanding of the tonal transitions between primary and complementary colours.

51 Spring Afternoon at Eragny: Grey Weather

Après-midi de printemps à Eragny: temps gris; 1898
oil on canvas, 60 x 73 cm
signed and dated lower left: 98
PV. 1035
Private Collection

Views across the meadow from his studio window at Eragny-sur-Epte were to provide an endless sequence of landscape motifs after Pissarro's move to the town in 1884, and especially in the 1890s. There are at least three variations of the view shown here made during 1898. Characteristic of the artist's awareness of the precise moment in a day, weather or season which the view denoted, each painting bears a supplementary title: 'Morning' (PV. 1034), 'November' (PV. 1061), and the one shown here, 'Grey Weather'. Such temporal precision was given not only to explain the specific tonal properties of each work, but also to imply a more systematic approach to the initial Impressionist programme of capturing landscape under a particular light condition. Pissarro had already attempted to impose a new order on Impressionism in the mid-1880s, when he briefly adopted the Neo-Impressionist procedures of Seurat and Signac [see cat. 47, 48]. However, more consistent brushwork and the subtle modulations between the different tones of green and grey in this work imply a debt to the pointillist application of paint characteristic of Neo-Impressionism and a greater understanding of the processes of transition (*passage*) between juxtaposed colours.

52 The Field by the Ango Inn, Varengeville

Le Clos de l'Auberge d'Ango, Varengeville; 1899
oil on canvas, 65 x 54 cm
signed and dated lower right: 99
PV. 1084
Private collection

Between September and October 1899
Pissarro stayed at Varengeville, on the
English Channel just south of Dieppe.
Here he produced a small group of
paintings which recorded the landscapes
around the two inns, l'Auberge d'Ango
and l'Auberge du Manoir (PV. 1083–1089).
As with the views across the meadows at
Eragny of the previous year [see cat. 51],
several of these paintings also make
specific reference to times of day and
weather conditions.

53 Pont-Neuf under Snow

Le Pont-Neuf sous la neige; 1901
oil on canvas, 59 x 80 cm
signed and dated lower right: 1901
PV. 1178
Private Collection

In November 1900 Pissarro rented an apartment at
28 Place Dauphine, at the downstream end of the
Ile de la Cité, Paris. From its windows he embarked
upon his fifth series of Parisian paintings. During the
previous decade, in part in response to Monet's series
paintings, starting with the Grainstacks of 1890–1, and
in part as a logical development of the Impressionist
concern to record the effects of changing light and
weather conditions on a single motif, Pissarro created
a sequence of series paintings. These series, however,
differed from Monet's in two significant respects. First,
their subject-matter was exclusively urban, recording
the ports of Rouen, Dieppe and Le Havre, and views of
Paris from the Boulevard Montmartre and the Avenue
de l'Opéra to the Tuileries Gardens. Second, each series
contained two or more sub-series, as Pissarro shifted
his angle of vision to create groups of views intended
to be seen in sequence. This view of the Pont-Neuf,
which looks towards the Right Bank of the Seine and
the recently constructed department store La Samari-
taine, constitutes one of three sub-series made by
Pissarro from his apartment windows on the Place
Dauphine. The other two look out due west across
the Square du Vert-Galant to the Louvre and the Grand
Palais, and pan south towards the Left Bank and the
Monnaie, to include the southern sector of the Square
du Vert-Galant.

PIERRE-AUGUSTE RENOIR

LIMOGES, 25 February 1841 – CAGNES, 3 December 1919

Renoir's family moved to Paris in 1844. After working in a firm of porcelain painters, Renoir started copying in the Louvre in 1860, and in 1862 he entered Gleyre's atelier. Here he met the future Impressionists Monet, Bazille and Sisley. He began to paint modern figure subjects and scenes drawn from contemporary life and in 1869, together with Monet, evolved the characteristic Impressionist technique at La Grenouillère, outside Paris. Intermittent success at the Salons persuaded Renoir, together with Monet, Degas, Pissarro and Sisley, to found an independent exhibition body in 1874. By the end of the 1870s, Renoir became increasingly uneasy with Impressionism's inability to create a more eternal image of nature. During the subsequent decade he travelled to the South of France, Italy and North Africa in search of new subjects and more brilliant colour, and began to execute a series of classicising nudes and monumental figures. He declined to exhibit at the eighth and final Impressionist exhibition (1886), preferring one-man shows. He settled permanently in the South of France in 1902.

The popularity of Renoir with Swiss collectors is illustrated by the fact that when the Kunstmuseum Winterthur mounted an important retrospective exhibition in 1935, all eighty works were borrowed from local collections. The exhibition was well received, and the concerns that the Winterthur public had expressed over the acquisition of a Renoir nude by the Kunstmuseum in 1917 had evidently been forgotten.

Arthur and Hedy Hahnloser of Winterthur bought their first Renoir, *La Fruitière* (c. 1900) in 1912. This acquisition was encouraged by their close friends, the artists Félix Vallotton and Henri Manguin, who described the painting as 'very lovely ... a significant painting, both in its dimensions as well as in its wonderful execution ...'(quoted in Luxembourg 1995, p. 77). When the Hahnloser Collection was shown at the Kunstmuseum Lucerne in 1940, it featured seventeen works by Renoir. Cuno Amiet apparently shared the enthusiasm of his fellow artists for Renoir, and encouraged Josef Müller of Solothurn to purchase Renoir's monumental *Bulgarian Blouse* through Galerie Paul Vallotton, Lausanne, in 1914. Müller had already

expressed an interest in Renoir's work, having seen a sample of it in an exhibition at the Künstlerhaus in Zurich in 1908. Sidney and Jenny Brown in Baden put together a remarkable collection of more than twenty Renoirs, the majority being purchased between 1909 and 1919, although a few further works were added in 1933 and 1940. Most of these were bought through the Paris dealer Ambroise Vollard. Consistent with the Browns' preference for small-scale paintings, the Renoirs in their collection were still-lifes, small landscapes and figure paintings, such as the delicate portrait of *Paul Meunier, fils Murer* (c. 1877), bought in 1909 and included by Carl Montag in the Grosse Ausstellung (Stuttgart, 1913), and a classicising study of Suzanne Valadon, *La Natte* (1884), purchased in December 1917, having been shown in the exhibition Französische Kunst des XIX. und XX. Jahrhunderts (October–November 1917).

From this exhibition's catalogue it may be surmised that either Emil Staub or Edouard Sturzenneger – or both of them – collected Renoirs.

Unlike other artists such as Cézanne, Gauguin and Van Gogh, Renoir was only given one retrospective exhibition in Switzerland before 1939. Despite this, his work was consistently in demand, entering almost all the major pioneering collections as well as those created after 1920 by, for example, Oskar Reinhart, Roger Firmenich, Bernhard Mayer, Arthur Wilhelm and E. G. Bührle. The large number of Renoirs in Swiss collections in part reflects the artist's own production, from the late 1870s, and specifically after 1900, of paintings which he regarded as destined specifically for the commercial market.

54 The Watering Place

L'Abreuvoir; 1873
oil on canvas, 47 x 61 cm
signed and dated lower right: 73
Private Collection

The loose, feathery brushwork laid over a smooth white ground recalls Renoir's early training as a porcelain painter in Paris between 1854 and 1858. Four years later he joined Gleyre's atelier, where he met the future Impressionists Monet, Sisley and Bazille. Unlike the first two, Renoir continued to make figure paintings throughout his career [see cat. 60, 61], but during the early 1870s, when Renoir was working out of doors according to Impressionist principles, he made a number of landscapes which were either devoid of figures, or in which figures play only a secondary role within the composition. This painting is transitional in style: the white ground gives a certain luminosity to the scene, but the use of black for areas of shadow, rather than the blues or violets adopted by this date by his fellow Impressionists, indicates that Renoir is still applying traditional rules of modelling rather than attempting to record light and shade through colour contrast.

55 The Rose Garden

La Roseraie; 1873
oil on canvas, 39.3 x 47.2 cm
signed lower left
Private Collection

This work, like *The Watering Place* [cat. 54], is an exercise in Impressionist techniques. The scudding clouds, the turbulent brushwork describing the rose bushes in the foreground, the dappled patterns of light and shade falling across the scene indicate that the painting is concerned with the translation into paint of a particular configuration of light as it falls upon the landscape. Whereas the overall tonality of *The Watering Place* was built up from a variety of greens and greys, the roses in the foreground here demand a far more intense hue.

The use of more intense colours can be found in other landscapes by Renoir painted around this time, for example, *Printemps à Chatou* (c. 1872–5, Private Collection).

56 Sunlit Landscape

Paysage ensoleillé; c. 1880
oil on canvas, 39 x 56 cm
signed lower right
Private Collection

The greater range of colour found in this landscape, together with the cursory indication of the trees, suggest that this work must be later in date than *The Watering Place* [cat. 54] and *The Rose Garden* [cat. 55]. However, the absence of intense colour and a more structured approach to brushwork indicate that the work must predate both Renoir's journey to North Africa in 1881 and his visit to Cézanne at L'Estaque in January 1882. It was while working with Cézanne in 1882, and again at La Roche-Guyon three years later, that Renoir finally began to apply his paint according to the directional principles that Cézanne had already developed [see cat. 5].

57 Still-Life: Pheasant in the Snow

Nature morte: le faisan sur la neige; 1879
oil on canvas, 49 x 64 cm
signed lower right
Private Collection

During the 1860s and '70s Renoir intermittently painted still-life subjects. In some instances a still-life formed part of a larger figure composition, as in *Bal du Moulin de la Galette* (1876, Musée d'Orsay, Paris) and *Portraits de Mme Charpentier et de ses filles* (1878, The Metropolitan Museum of Art, New York); others were planned as independent works, as, for example, *Nature morte: fleurs* (1864, Kunsthalle, Hamburg), *Nature morte au bouquet* (1871, The Museum of Fine Arts, Houston), and the work shown here. The awkward placing of the pheasant on the ground, with the snow acting as a backdrop, suggests that the painting must have been executed in the studio. Why Renoir should have wished to show the dead bird out of doors is unclear. He was, perhaps, recalling Gustave Courbet's paintings of dead game laid out in landscapes made in the later 1850s and '60s rather than the more recent studies of Bazille, Monet, Sisley and Caillebotte.

58 Still-Life: Fish

Nature morte: les poissons; 1915
oil on canvas, 35 x 56 cm
signed lower left
Museum zu Allerheiligen, Schaffhausen

Increasingly crippled by arthritis during the closing years of his life, Renoir turned to subjects which could be executed in the studio: figure subjects, portraits and still-lifes. In the late 1890s he had recommended that Julie Manet should paint such subjects, 'in order to teach yourself to paint quickly'. The sureness of the long, gestural strokes to define the fish in this still-life illustrates this point. Renoir also recognised that still-lifes, like other small, informal paintings of landscapes and figures, were in demand from collectors, both in France and abroad. This work was purchased by Oskar Reinhart of Winterthur who entrusted most of his collection to the foundation established at his home, Am Römerholz. Some of the works in the collection remained with members of the family; others were given away, as was this work to the Schaffhausen Museum in 1944.

59 Woman with a Rose

Femme à la rose; c.1876
oil on canvas, 35.5 x 27 cm
signed lower right
D.167
Fondation Rau pour le Tiers-Monde, Zurich

During the 1870s Renoir produced a
number of commercially successful
paintings of fashionable beautiful young
women. Rather than being portraits of
specific sitters, they tended to show
women at the theatre in the company of a
male companion (*La Loge*, 1874, Courtauld
Institute Galleries, London; *Dans la loge*,
c.1874, Private Collection), seated in a café
(*Au Café*, c.1877, Rijksmuseum Kröller-
Müller, Otterlo), or single figures braiding
their hair (*La Chevelure*, 1876, National
Gallery of Art, Washington DC). Although
both the format and the technique of
the painting shown here, as well as the
somewhat coquettish glance of the young
girl, relate it to this group of works, the
absence of any identifiable setting or
activity suggests that it may be a portrait
of an unidentified sitter.

60 Nude Seated by the Sea

Nue au bord de la mer; 1890–5
oil on canvas, 54.5 x 40 cm
signed lower left
Private Collection

Towards the end of the 1870s, Renoir, like
Monet and Pissarro, experienced increasing
unease with the tenets of High Impressionism.
In 1881 he spent three months in Italy, studying
classical Antiquity and the art of the Renaissance,
notably the work of Raphael. In later life, he told
Jacques-Emile Blanche of his admiration for
Raphael: 'Raphael broke with the schools of his
time, dedicated himself to the antique, to
grandeur and eternal beauty.' It was precisely
these qualities which Renoir sought to instil
into his own work, transforming the ephemeral
qualities of Impressionism into an art which
could stand beside that of the Old Masters.

Renoir returned from Italy with a study of
a nude bather, *Baigneuse blonde* (1881, Sterling
and Francine Clark Art Institute, Williamstown).
In pose and technique the work marked a new
point of departure in his treatment of this
subject. It is the first of a long line of bathers
created over the following three decades, which
include both the great *Baigneuses* of 1887 (Philadelphia Museum of Art) and works such as the
one shown here.

The nudes of the 1880s tend to be executed
in a rather dry, linear technique. In those of
the subsequent decade Renoir adopted a softer
technique, applying the paint more loosely.
In all these works there is little relationship
between figure and background, and the nudes
remain untouched by any play of light,
confirming that they were painted in the studio.

61 Portrait of a Young Woman

Portrait d'une jeune femme; 1901
oil on canvas, 65 x 54 cm
signed upper right
Private Collection

More than Monet, Pissarro or Sisley, Renoir shared with Cézanne and Gustave Caillebotte a fascination with depicting the human form, including portraiture. He worked in this genre throughout his life, with the exception of a brief interlude at the end of the 1880s. Most of his sitters were women, many of them society ladies.

After 1900 Renoir handled his tonal range with extreme sophistication, marrying appropriate hues to different subjects. The use of soft, modulated tones broken by stronger colours in this portrait appears to have been chosen to convey the femininity of the sitter.

ALFRED SISLEY

PARIS, 30 October 1839 – MORET-SUR-LOING, 29 January 1899

Sisley was born in Paris of English parents. He was sent to London to embark on a career in business, but returned to Paris and entered Gleyre's atelier in 1862 where he met the future members of the Impressionist group, Monet, Renoir and Bazille. Throughout the 1860s, Sisley produced landscapes in a style influenced by Corot, Courbet and the Barbizon School painter Daubigny. After 1870, however, he adopted Monet's Impressionist technique and began to paint landscapes near his homes at Louveciennes and Marly-le-Roi and along the River Seine. He visited England in 1874. In 1882 he settled permanently at Moret-sur-Loing. Sisley showed at the first six Impressionist exhibitions. Unlike his fellow Impressionists, he experienced public recognition only late in his life, with one-man exhibitions at Durand-Ruel in 1883 and at Georges Petit in 1897.

On 7 April 1910, Dr Georges Viau wrote to Sidney Brown informing him of the imminent arrival in Baden of twelve paintings, one of which was Alfred Sisley's late *The Church at Moret - Rainy Weather, Morning* (1893), one of fifteen studies of this subject. As with so many of these early purchases, Brown had been advised by Carl Montag. He never acquired another example of Sisley's work. Three years later, Montag's advocacy of Sisley was expressed in a letter dated 17 January 1913, addressed to Gustav Tanner. The Zurich dealer Tanner was negotiating a relationship with the Bernheim-Jeune Gallery in Paris and laying plans for future exhibitions. Montag encouraged Tanner to consider exhibitions devoted to Monet, Sisley, Morisot, d'Espagnat, Durenne, Bonnard, Signac and Marquet (Gloor 1985b, p. 175).

Despite relatively strong representations in the early exhibitions devoted to French modern art held in Basel, Zurich and Winterthur, few works by Sisley entered the major pioneering collections. The Hahnlosers showed no interest in his work, nor did Georg Reinhart. However, Hans Sulzer and Oskar Reinhart included his work in their collections, the latter buying two excellent examples, *The Canal St Martin* (1870; D. 17) and *The Aqueduct of Louveciennes* (1876; D. 213); and Emil Staub-Terlinden of Männedorf owned *The Bridge of St Cloud* (1877; D. 255).

Today, many works by Sisley are to be found in Swiss collections. Of the series of the *Eglise de Moret*, four of the fifteen paintings are in Switzerland, one in the Langmatt Stiftung, Baden, one in the Kunstmuseum Winterthur and two in private hands.

62 Regatta at Hampton Court

Les Régates à Hampton Court; 1874
oil on canvas, 46 x 61 cm
signed lower left
D. 125
Private Collection

Sisley had lived in London in 1857–9, when training to take up a career in business. He returned as a painter in July 1874, staying briefly in the City before moving to Hampton Court on the River Thames. Here he undertook a series of paintings which provide a visual map of the area from Hampton Court Palace upstream to Molesley Weir and Tagg's Island.

This view was painted from the riverside terrace of the Castle Inn which lay at the southern end of the bridge spanning the Thames. It shows the northern bank with the Tudor brick stables at the western end of Hampton Court Palace; the bridge lies immediately beyond the left-hand edge of the canvas. The regatta shown here started in 1867, on a course downstream from Hampton Court Bridge to Thames Ditton. The other regatta, founded in 1873, covered a course above the bridge from Molesley Weir to Tagg's Island, and was also recorded by Sisley (*The Regatta at Molesley*, 1874, Musée d'Orsay, Paris; D. 126).

In keeping with Sisley's exploration of a given location, the same river bank, stable block and flag pole, seen from a slightly different angle, appear in a dramatic view under the arches of Hampton Court Bridge (*Under Hampton Court Bridge*, 1874, Kunstmuseum Winterthur, presented by Dr H. Wolfer; D. 142). Likewise, the same river bank, complete with flag pole, has been extended upstream to include the end of Hampton Court Bridge and the Mitre Inn in *Le Pont de Hampton Court – The Mitre Inn* (1874, Wallraf-Richartz-Museum, Cologne; D. 123).

63 Snow at Louveciennes

La Neige à Louveciennes; 1874
oil on canvas, 65 x 92 cm
signed and dated lower right: 74
D. 148
Private Collection

Sisley had settled in Louveciennes, a village lying to the west of Paris between Bougival and St Germain-en-Laye, probably in the spring of 1871, to escape the Paris Commune. He remained here until the winter of 1874–5, when he moved up the road to Marly-le-Roi.

While in Louveciennes he painted extensively in the village and its environs, including Port-Marly and Bougival. This view shows the outskirts of the village. As with his paintings of the Thames at Hampton Court, Sisley's views of Louveciennes demonstrate a visual exploration of a known landscape in which knowledge of what lies beyond the edge of a canvas, or over the horizon of a composition, is seemingly implied.

The Impressionists frequently took up the challenge of painting snowscapes, since the tonal values of such scenes lent themselves to a direct translation of light and shadow into hues of yellow and blue/mauve tinted zones, as applied here, in defiance of the traditional use of white for highlight and black for shadow.

HENRI DE TOULOUSE-LAUTREC

ALBI, 24 November 1864 – CHATEAU DE MALROMÉ, GIRONDE, 9 September 1901

Known as much for his experimental lithography as for his paintings, Toulouse-Lautrec was born into an aristocratic family. Accidents during his childhood left him deformed. After informal lessons with the horse-painter Princeteau, Toulouse-Lautrec joined Bonnat's atelier in Paris in 1882, and that of Cormon in 1884 where he met Bernard, Anquetin and Van Gogh, three artists who were shortly to reject naturalist painting. In 1884 he took an atelier in Montmartre and from then on drew heavily upon the local scenes of prostitution and popular entertainment, such as cabarets, circuses and *café-concerts*, for his paintings and lithographs. Toulouse-Lautrec exhibited his work primarily with independent exhibition bodies such as Les XX, Brussels (1890), the Salon des Indépendants, Paris (from 1890), and the gallery Le Barc de Boutteville (from 1891). In 1902 a retrospective exhibition of his work was shown in the Salon des Indépendants.

Whereas Hodler does not appear to have exhibited in an international exhibition beside Toulouse-Lautrec until the Berlin Secession of 1909 devoted to graphic work, Félix Vallotton figured with Lautrec in exhibitions as early as 1891 in the Salon des Indépendants, Paris. Given the influential position held by Vallotton among the early collectors in Winterthur, it is hardly surprising to find several of them acquiring works by Lautrec. Georg Reinhart was probably the first to purchase a work by him. On 18 May 1914 he bought *Femme se coiffant* (DP. 391) through Carl Montag in Paris. Some ten years later, Georg Reinhart's brother Oskar bought a magnificent work, *La Clownesse* (DP. 589), which had previously been owned by Bernheim-Jeune. Neither brother acquired any further works by Lautrec, but the Hahnlosers established an important position for the artist within their own collection, owning some five works, including *Portrait d'homme* (1883), *La Goulue et Valentin le désossé* (1890) and *The Card Game* (1893). Winterthur's enthusiasm for Lautrec can also be seen in the fact that the two important Swiss exhibitions of his work before 1939 were held in that city, in 1924 and 1929. Beyond Winterthur, neither the Browns nor the Staechelins considered his art appropriate to their collections. Richard Kisling, however, in Zurich, does appear to have owned at least two works which he lent to the Zurich Kunsthaus exhibition, Französische Kunst des XIX. und XX. Jahrhunderts, in 1917 (nos. 238 and 241).

The continued interest in Switzerland in Toulouse-Lautrec is witnessed in exhibitions held in Zurich in 1943, followed by others mounted over the following decade in Basel, Bern and Zurich. Supported by dealers such as Nathan and Feilchenfeldt in Zurich, a younger generation of collectors began acquiring his works. Emil Georg Bührle, for example, bought three major works between 1951 and 1954 and, reflecting the more international nature of the Swiss art market, he purchased them in Paris and New York, as well as in Zurich.

cat. 64

64 In the Garden (Woman Seated in a Garden)

Sous la verdure (Femme assise dans un jardin); 1890–1
oil on panel, 55 x 46 cm
signed lower left
DP. 409
Private Collection

65 Prostitute: The Sphinx

Femme de maison, la Sphynge; 1898 or earlier
'peinture à l'essence' on cardboard, 68.5 x 47 cm
signed and dated lower left: 1898
DP. 665
Private Collection (Courtesy of Walter Feilchenfeldt)

Around 1890 Lautrec produced a small number of portraits set not in interiors but in the Paris garden of the photographer Forest. Possibly prompted by the rampant vegetation in the garden, Lautrec painted these portraits in predominantly green tonalities and their complementary colour, purple. All the sitters are placed in relaxed, if somewhat eccentric poses in the garden which is transformed into a purely decorative backdrop.

Lautrec's interest in figures placed in garden settings dates back to the early 1880s and is seen in works such as *La Jeune Routy à Celeyran* (1882, Bayerische Staatsgemäldesammlungen, Neue Pinakothek, Munich) and the *Comtesse A. de Toulouse-Lautrec* (1884, Museu de Arte de São Paulo). However, unlike the broad, graphic brushwork and exaggerated palette of these later works, those of the early 1880s, with their rather square brushwork and subdued palette, show the influence of Jules Bastien-Lepage.

Throughout much of the 1890s Lautrec painted portraits of prostitutes, or *femmes de maison*. While many of these have been dated to 1894, the one shown here probably dates from slightly later. Although dated by Lautrec '1898' this may record the year it was sold – or possibly given – to its first owner, Louis Bouglé, who in 1896 had commissioned from Lautrec the poster for 'La Chaîne Simpson'.

Whatever the profession of the sitter – she may have been a studio model rather than a specific *femme de maison* – she is presented as a monumental, almost heroic figure, with her profile turned slightly towards the spectator and her torso draped like an Antique bust. The deftness of the drawing and the schematic colour laid in thinly over the cardboard support have all the characteristics of Lautrec's draughtsmanship, which was as much in evidence in his lithographs as in his paintings.

66 The Two Friends

L'Abandon, ou Les Deux Amies; 1895
'peinture à l'essence' on cardboard,
45.5 x 67.5 cm
signed lower left
DP. 598
Private Collection

From 1891 Lautrec had frequented the brothels of the
Rue des Moulins and the Rue d'Amboise, recording
with acute sensitivity and understanding the lives of
their female inmates, most notably in his suite of
lithographs *Elles* (1896). In this painting, he depicts a
moment of sexual intimacy in a lesbian relationship,
a relationship that he treated with great sympathy;
a langorous atmosphere is suggested by the two
reclining figures. The fluency of the blocking-in of the
figures and surrounding space suggests that this work
was made directly from life. However, preliminary
studies for both the figures, modified in the final composition, confirm that it was composed from models
posed in the studio. An extra strip of cardboard was
added on the left, suggesting that the composition
required more space for the figures.

67 Two Knights in Armour

Deux Chevaliers en armure; c. 1900
oil on canvas, 65 x 81 cm
signed with monogram lower left
DP. 663
Private Collection

At the end of his life, Lautrec turned to historical subjects, drawing his inspiration from opera, notably de Lara's *Messaline*, a production of which opened on 14 December 1900 at the Grand Théâtre, Bordeaux. Lautrec was permitted to sketch in the wings of the theatre, creating a group of dramatically lit, dark works with an eccentric viewpoint showing figures in Roman costumes and stage sets. While the present painting does not share the dark tones of the *Messaline* group, the imaginative evocation of a past age, in this case the Middle Ages, would suggest it was painted in the final period of the artist's career.

VINCENT VAN GOGH

GROOT ZUNDERT, NORTH BRABANT, 30 March 1853 – AUVERS, 29 July 1890

Son of a Dutch minister, Van Gogh took up painting *c*. 1880, after working as an art dealer, a teacher and a missionary. Following a brief period working under Mauve at The Hague in 1883, Van Gogh travelled to Antwerp in the winter of 1885–6. He joined his brother, Theo, in Paris in March 1886. He studied at Cormon's atelier, where he met Toulouse-Lautrec and Emile Bernard, but also absorbed Impressionism and Neo-Impressionism, which, combined with his admiration for Japanese prints, encouraged him to adopt an increasingly brilliant palette and dramatic technique and create more strongly patterned compositions. He left Paris for Arles, Provence, in February 1888, intending to establish a colony of painters. Gauguin joined him in October 1888, staying until Van Gogh suffered a breakdown in December. From May 1889 to May 1890 Van Gogh lived in the hospital at St Rémy, near Arles, moving from there to Auvers in Northern France, where he killed himself in July 1890. Van Gogh's paintings became increasingly decorative in their use of colour, boldly drawn outline and thickly laid-on paint.

———————————————

Van Gogh's first exhibition in Switzerland was held in July 1908 at the Künstlerhaus Zurich, but his work was already known to artists such as Cuno Amiet, Hodler and Félix Vallotton who belonged to the international avant-garde and acted as advisers to several of the leading pioneer collectors. Hodler's work was exhibited at the Berlin Secession in 1903 beside that of Van Gogh, and again in 1906 in Bremen at the Kunstverein's Internationale Ausstellung. As early as 1891 Vallotton's work was included in exhibitions which also showed work by Van Gogh, including the Salon des Indépendants, Paris. Although Cuno Amiet did not exhibit beside Van Gogh until 1908 in the Künstlerhaus Zurich, his art, which bridged Fauvism and Expressionism, was influenced by Van Gogh and he was acknowledged by many contemporary critics to have formed the taste of the early collectors in Switzerland.

Van Gogh's painting *Two Children* (1890; F.784) was included in an exhibition of predominantly Hague School artists at the Künstlerhaus Zurich, 11 April–12 May 1907. According to Gloor (p. 300, n. 828), it was purchased by Richard Kisling from C. M. van Gogh of Amsterdam on 17 May 1907. However, it was the impact of the first exhibition to include a significant group of Van Gogh's works in Switzerland held at the Künstlerhaus Zurich from 10 to 26 July 1908 which played a decisive role in the history of Swiss taste. Forty-one paintings were exhibited, and pioneer collectors purchased either directly from the exhibition, such as Hans Schuler, who bought one work, and Fritz Meyer-Fierz, who bought four, or shortly after, as did Richard Kisling, who purchased *Young Girl Standing against a Background of Wheat* (1890; F.788) through Bollag et Cie (cat. no. 40 in that exhibition; Chester Dale Collection, National Gallery of Art, Washington DC). Other early collectors, including Josef Müller and his sister, Gertrud, visited the exhibition; within six months each had acquired a work by the artist [see cat. 71]. Thereafter, works by Van Gogh entered such major collections as those of Arthur and Hedy Hahnloser, which, when shown at Lucerne in 1940, included thirteen Van Goghs [see cat. 72]; Rudolf Staechelin [see cat. 68] and Oskar Reinhart. After 1908, Van Gogh was included in group exhibitions in Zurich (1917), Winterthur (1922) and Bern (1934), and a major retrospective exhibition consisting of ninety-nine paintings was shown at the Kunsthaus Zurich from 3 July to 10 August 1924, followed three years later by another exhibition at the Kunsthalle, Basel. Such regular exposure, together with the example of the pioneering collectors, encouraged younger collectors to acquire works by the artist, a pattern which persists to this day.

68 Path through a Field with Willows

late spring 1888
oil on canvas, 32.5 x 40.3 cm
F. 407
Private Collection

Van Gogh moved from Paris to Arles in February 1888. On 7 May he wrote to his brother, Theo: 'There is a little landscape with a hovel, white, red and green, and a cypress beside it; you have the drawing of it, and I did the whole painting of it in the house. This will show you that, if you like, I can make little pictures like Japanese prints of all these drawings' (Letter 484). The highly finished drawing (F.1499) to which Vincent refers is dated in his own hand: '*Arles Mars 88*'; this suggests a *terminus ante quem* for the painting shown here.

Vincent's assertion that he can make 'little pictures like the Japanese prints' alludes to his own enthusiasm for coloured Japanese woodblock prints, of which he owned a significant number. It is also a statement of his determination to move beyond the mere translation of such prints into paintings, as he had done in Paris during 1887, and to transform the landscape of southern France into their visual equivalents. That he believed such a transformation possible can be seen in his decision to leave Paris in order to settle in the south in a warm, luminous landscape which he could equate with the vision of Japan he had formed from his own collection of prints. In a letter to the artist Emile Bernard he proclaimed of Arles: '... this country seems to me to be as beautiful as Japan as far as the limpid quality of the atmosphere and the gay colour effects are concerned' (Letter B2).

69 Sunny Lawn in a Public Park (Arles)

1888
oil on canvas, 60.5 x 73.5 cm
F. 428
Private Collection

Van Gogh refers to this painting in three letters of 12 July, early August and 3 September 1888. He emphasises that it shows 'a garden without flowers, that is to say, a lawn newly mown, bright green with grey hay spread in long streaks' (Letter W5; c. 1 August 1888). The reference to the absence of flowers in this painting distinguishes it from two near contemporaneous works representing a garden in Arles full of flowers (F. 429 and 430).

In the letter of 12 July Vincent states that the composition has only 'a little corner of blue sky at the top' (Letter 508). The painting shares with the two views of a flower garden an exaggeratedly high horizon line which effectively flattens out the composition, making it more decorative than descriptive, in keeping with the principles of Japanese prints.

70 The Garden of St Paul's Hospital

1889
pencil, chalk and watercolour on paper,
46.5 x 61.5 cm
F. 1536
Private Collection

Van Gogh left Arles on 8 May 1889 to take up residence in St Paul's Asylum at St Rémy. This watercolour shows the garden of the asylum [see cat. 71]. It was originally dated to spring 1890, but its subject-matter and graphic style suggest that it should be placed in the summer of the previous year.

Van Gogh moved from St Rémy to Auvers, to be in the care of Dr Gachet, in May 1890 [see cat. 73].

71 Portrait of Trabuc, an Attendant of St Paul's Hospital, St Rémy

1889
oil on canvas, 61 x 46 cm
F. 629
Kunstmuseum Solothurn, Dübi-Müller-Foundation

Following a severe illness in July and August 1889, Van Gogh took up painting again in early September, making a landscape (F. 625), two self-portraits (F. 626 and 627), this portrait of Trabuc and one of his wife (F. 631). In a letter to his brother, Theo, of around 4–5 September 1889 he wrote '... it is more than time I did a little figure work' (Letter 604).

Trabuc worked as an orderly at the Hospital of St Paul, in St Rémy, and his demeanour had attracted Vincent. He seemed to combine the character of a Spanish grandee and something of the military, the latter quality suggested by 'his small, quick, black eyes' (Letter 605). While the neatness of Trabuc's silhouette suggests a certain military precision, the black and white stripes of his orderly's uniform seem to refer back to the monochrome palette of Velázquez. Trabuc's almost fully frontal, half-length pose is one which Vincent used regularly for his sitters, for example for the *Portrait of Dr Rey* (1889, Pushkin Museum, Moscow; F. 500) and *Patience Escalier* (1888, Private Collection; F. 444).

The portrait of Trabuc must have been completed by 10 September when Vincent wrote to Theo that he had made a duplicate of the work for him (Letter 605). Since the original painting was given to the sitter, the work shown here is almost certainly that duplicate; it was acquired in April 1908 by Gertrud Dübi-Müller of Solothurn, sister of Josef Müller, thus making it the first work by Van Gogh to enter a Swiss collection.

72 Peasant Woman against a Background of Wheat

late June 1890
oil on canvas, 92 x 73 cm
F. 774
Private Collection

This painting must have been finished by 1 July 1890: in a letter of that date addressed to Theo, Vincent describes the work as a 'sketch' rather than as a finished painting and comments that he fears it is 'a bit coarse': 'Here are three sketches [the other two were *The Château d'Auvers*, F.770; and *Undergrowth with Two Figures*, F. 773] – one of a peasant woman, big yellow hat with a knot of sky-blue ribbons, very red face, rich blue blouse with orange spots, background of ears of wheat. It is a size 30 canvas, but I am afraid it is really a bit coarse' (letter 646).

This painting of a peasant girl represents an interesting fusion between two artistic concerns explored in Vincent's last months at Auvers: the large-scale, single figure, half- or full-length, strongly outlined and placed close to the picture plane – for example, *Madeleine Gachet at the Piano* (1890; F.772) and *Portrait of Dr Gachet* (1890; F.753) – and the study of nature, be it garden flowers or ears of wheat. Between 16 and 23 June 1890, Vincent wrote to Paul Gauguin saying that he was 'trying to do some studies of wheat ... nothing but ears of wheat with green-blue stalks...' but was finding that he 'cannot draw it' (Letter 643). He wanted to use such studies as a backdrop against which he would 'like to paint some portraits', seeing the variety of greens in the ripening wheat as the source of tonal vibrations which establish a visual equivalent to 'the gentle rustle of the ears swaying in the breeze ...'. Such an exercise was attempted in the painting shown here and in a variant which shows the same model virtually full length against a similar background: *Young Girl Standing against a Background of Wheat* (1890; F.788).

This painting was acquired by Arthur and Hedy Hahnloser in 1920.

73 Daubigny's Garden with a Black Cat (July)

July 1890
oil on canvas, 56 x 101.5 cm
F. 777
Rudolf Staechelin Family Foundation
(on loan to the Kunstmuseum Basel)

This is one of two paintings of a view across a garden towards a house once owned by Charles Daubigny, the Barbizon landscape painter (the other is F. 776). From the moment of his arrival in Auvers-sur-Oise in May 1890, it would appear that Vincent had intended to paint such a subject (Letter 642); a smaller, square canvas made before 17 June 1890 shows a corner of the older painter's garden (F. 765): 'I am planning to make a more important canvas of Daubigny's house and garden, of which I have already done a little study' (Letter 642).

Despite the radical nature of Vincent's art of the last two years of his life, his work remained deeply impregnated with direct and indirect references to earlier painters. While direct references are found in his reworkings of compositions by Delacroix, J.F. Millet and Gustave Doré, he also paid homage to earlier masters by using similar subject-matter or treatment, as in *The Fields (Auvers)* [cat. 73] or by choosing a subject with links to earlier painters, as in the paintings of Daubigny's garden. In these, Vincent

acknowledges the significant contribution made by Daubigny to the evolution of modern landscape painting in France.

This version of the composition initially belonged to 'Père' Julien Tanguy, the colour merchant and unofficial dealer for artists including Cézanne and Emile Bernard. It was shown in Basel in 1906 and entered the Rudolf Staechelin Collection by 1917 via the Galerie Paul Vallotton, Lausanne, founded in 1913 in association with the Paris dealer Bernheim-Jeune.

74 The Fields (Auvers)

1890
oil on canvas, 64 x 80 cm
F. 761
Private Collection
(Courtesy of Walter Feilchenfeldt)

Vincent came to live in Auvers-sur-Oise in May 1890 under the care of Dr Gachet, a homeopathic doctor and friend of Camille Pissarro and Paul Cézanne, who was also a collector and amateur printmaker [see cat. 3]. Van Gogh's move from the southern landscapes of Arles and St Rémy to the north did not affect his choice of subject-matter: in the expansive views of the chalklands surrounding Auvers, he still referred back to landscape traditions of the earlier 19th century and of 17th-century Dutch art.

In this painting, the broad expanse of the plain, crowned by a dramatic sky, evokes the wide horizons of works by Koninck and Ruysdael. That Vincent viewed such sources through the mediation of his more immediate precursors is evident from his remark about a similar landscape, *The Plain of Auvers* (1890,

Österreichische Staatsgalerie, Vienna; F. 775), which, he declared, was similar in composition to works of the early 19th-century French landscapist Georges Michel: 'Then the horizontal landscape with fields, like one of Michel's...' (Letter 646; c. 1 July 1890).

BIBLIOGRAPHY

This bibliography is organised as follows:
I. GENERAL LITERATURE
II. COLLECTING REGIONS
III. PRIVATE COLLECTORS
Entries are arranged chronologically within each subsection.
The bibliography was compiled and arranged by Franziska Baetcke.

I. GENERAL LITERATURE

I.1. *General Literature about Private Collections in Switzerland*

A. Bréal, 'Le goût de la peinture française en Suisse', in *La Suisse et les Français*, ed. by A. Castell, Paris 1920, pp. 223–32.

P. Courthion, 'L'Art Français dans les Collections privées en Suisse', *L'Amour de l'Art*, VII/1–2, 1926, pp. 1–68.

G. Jedlicka, 'Vom privaten und vom öffentlichen Sammeln', *Das Werk*, XXXI, 1944, pp. 274–7.

P. Cabanne, *Le roman des grands collectionneurs*, Paris 1961.

D. Cooper and K. Clark, *Great Private Collections*, London 1963.

D.E. Gordon, *Modern Art Exhibitions 1900–1916, Selected Catalogue Documentation*, 2 vols., Munich 1974.

New York 1976. *European Master Paintings from Swiss Collections, Post-Impressionism to World War II*, exhibition catalogue by J. Elderfield, New York, Museum of Modern Art, 1976.

H. Keller, 'Art Museums at Winterthur', *Apollo*, CX/212 (New Series), 1979, pp. 293–301.

L. Marfurt-Elmiger, *Der Schweizerische Kunstverein 1806–1981, Ein Beitrag zur schweizerischen Kulturgeschichte*, Bern 1981 (with detailed bibliography).

L. Gloor, 'Die "permanenten Ausstellungen" und der Kunsthandel in der Schweiz im 19. Jahrhundert', *Zeitschrift für Schweizerische Archäologie und Kunstgeschichte*, no. 43/1, 1986, pp. 387–90.

L. Gloor, *Von Böcklin zu Cézanne, Die Rezeption des französischen Impressionismus in der deutschen Schweiz*, Bern, Frankfurt a.M. and New York 1986 (the essential text to the subject, including detailed bibliography).

'Das Tor zur Moderne, Paul Cézanne in Schweizer Sammlungen', *Du, Die Zeitschrift der Kultur*, no. 9, 1989 (special issue devoted to Cézanne in Swiss collections).

Luxembourg 1995. *Luxe, Calme et Volupté, Regards sur le Post-Impressionnisme, Collectionneurs à Winterthur et Baden au début du XXᵉ siècle*, exhibition catalogue, Luxembourg, Casino, 1995.

I.2. *Catalogues of the Most Important Exhibitions of Impressionist Art in Switzerland*

Basel 1906. *Exposition d'Art français*, exhibition catalogue, Basel, Kunsthalle, March–April 1906.

Zurich 1908. *Französische Impressionisten*, exhibition catalogue, Zurich, Kunsthaus, October–November 1908.

Basel 1908. *November-Ausstellung 1908*, exhibition catalogue, Basel, Kunsthalle, 1908.

Basel 1909. *Salon français de Bâle, 1ᵉʳᵉ Exposition, Marc-Dardonville*, exhibition catalogue, Basel, Kunsthalle, November 1909.

Basel 1910. *II. Salon français de Bâle*, exhibition catalogue, Basel, Kunsthalle, October 1910.

Zurich 1911. *Katalog der Ausstellung Dezember 1911*, exhibition catalogue, Zurich, Kunsthaus, 1911 (mainly French Impressionists).

Basel 1912. *Januar-Ausstellung 1912, Französische Impressionisten*, exhibition catalogue, Basel, Kunsthalle, 1912.

Zurich 1912. *Ausstellung von Werken Paul Gauguins*, exhibition catalogue, Zurich, Kunstsalon Wolfsberg, March–April 1912.

Zurich 1913. *Ausstellung französischer Kunst*, exhibition catalogue, Zurich, Kunsthaus, February–March 1913.

Basel 1913. *Oktober-Ausstellung, Französische Meister*, exhibition catalogue, Basel, Kunsthalle, 1913 (mainly French Impressionists).

Zurich 1915. *Ausstellung Januar/Februar*, exhibition catalogue, Zurich, Kunsthaus, 1915 (French Art).

Basel 1915. *Mai-Ausstellung, Französische Klassiker des 19. Jahrhunderts*, exhibition catalogue, Basel, Kunsthalle, 1915 (mainly French Impressionists).

Zurich 1915. *Ausstellung Juli/August*, exhibition catalogue, Zurich, 1915 (French Art).

Basel 1916. *Mai-Ausstellung, Französische Maler*, exhibition catalogue, Basel, Kunsthalle, 1916.

Basel 1917. *Exposition de Peinture française*, exhibition catalogue, Basel, Kunsthalle, January 1917 (mainly French Impressionists).

Zurich 1917. *Französische Kunst des XIX. und XX. Jahrhunderts, Verzeichnis der ausgestellten Werke*, exhibition catalogue, Zurich, Kunsthaus, 1917.

Basel 1918. *Auguste Rodin, 1840–1917, Exposition de sculptures, aquarelles, dessins et estampes originales du maître, organisée par la Société des amis des arts de Bâle et le Musée Rodin*, exhibition catalogue, Basel, Kunsthalle, 1918.

Geneva 1918. *Catalogue des tableaux, dessins et sculptures de l'Ecole française du XIXᵉ siècle*, exhibition catalogue, Geneva, Musée d'Art et d'Histoire, 1918.

Basel 1924. *Vincent von Gogh*, exhibition catalogue, Basel, Kunsthalle, 1924.

Paris 1938. *La Peinture française du XIXᵉ siècle en Suisse*, exhibition catalogue with an introduction by H. Hahnloser-Bühler, Paris, Galerie des Beaux-Arts, 1938.

Paris 1959. *De Géricault à Matisse, Chefs-d'œuvre français des collections suisses*, exhibition catalogue, Paris, Petit Palais, with the collaboration of C. Montag, 1959.

Lausanne 1964. *Chefs-d'œuvre des collections suisses de Manet à Picasso*, exhibition catalogue, Lausanne, Palais de Beaulieu, 1964 (mainly identical with the exhibition shown in Paris, Orangerie des Tuileries, 1967, with separate catalogue).

Lausanne 1984. *L'Impressionnisme dans les collections romandes*, exhibition catalogue, Lausanne, Fondation de l'Hermitage, 1984.

I.3. *Texts about Impressionism/Influential Critics*

R. Muther, *Ein Jahrhundert französischer Malerei*, Berlin 1901.

J. Meier-Graefe, *Entwicklungsgeschichte der modernen Kunst, Vergleichende Betrachtung der bildenden Künste als Beitrag zur modernen Ästhetik*, Stuttgart 1904 (reeditions ²1914, ³1924).

H.G. Kessler, *Impressionisten, Die Begründer der modernen Malerei*, Munich 1908.

T. Duret, *Les peintres impressionnistes, Pissarro, Claude Monet, Sisley, Renoir, Berthe Morisot, Cézanne, Guillaumin*, Paris 1878 (German edition *Die Impressionisten*, Berlin 1908, ²1914, ³1918, ⁴1920, ⁵1923).

J. Widmer, 'Die neuere Malerei in der Schweiz', *Kunst und Künstler*, VIII, 1909/10, pp. 147–60.

J. Winkler, *Mißstände in der Schweizerischen Kunstpflege*, Bern 1911.

W. Wartmann, 'Kunstsammlung und Kunstausstellung', *Das Kunsthaus*, II, 1912, pp. 13–17.

W. Barth, 'Zur Verständigung über moderne Kunst, Ein Vorwort', *Beiträge zur zeitgenössischen Kunst*, ed. by Basler Kunstverein, I/3, 1917.

W. Schäfer, *Die moderne Malerei in der deutschen Schweiz*, Frauenfeld-Leipzig 1924.

W. Wartmann, 'La Suisse et l'art français', in *La Peinture française du XIXe siècle en Suisse*, exhibition catalogue, Paris, Galerie des Beaux-Arts, 1938, unpaginated.

G. Schmidt, 'La Suisse et la Peinture française du XIXe siècle et du XXe siècle', *Revue économique franco-suisse*, XXXIII, 1954, pp. 345–9.

P. Courthion, *Charles Montag, Winterthour, 23 mars 1880–28 juillet 1956* [1956].

K. Moffett, *Meier-Graefe as art critic*, Munich 1973.

Winterthur 1980–81. Karl Montag, Winterthur, Kunstmuseum, 1980–81 (an information sheet was published on the occasion of the exhibition).

Baden 1992. *Carl Montag, Maler und Kunstvermittler (1880–1956)*, exhibition catalogue by F. Deuchler, Baden, Stiftung 'Langmatt', 1992.

I.4. Art Dealers

P. Cassirer, 'Krieg und Kunst', *Die weissen Blätter*, V, 1918, p. 155.

F. Nathan, *Erinnerungen aus meinem Leben*, Zurich 1965.

F. Nathan and P. Nathan, ed., *Dr. Fritz Nathan und Dr. Peter Nathan, 1922–1972*, Zurich 1972.

A. Vollard, *Souvenirs d'un marchand de tableaux*, Paris 1937.

Lucerne 1988. *Von Matisse bis Picasso, Hommage an Siegfried Rosengart*, exhibition catalogue, Lucerne, Kunstmuseum, 1988.

Madrid 1989. *Colección Beyeler*, exhibition catalogue, Madrid, Centro de Arte Reina Sofía, 1989 (supplement to the exhibition catalogue with texts in English, Basel 1989).

II. IMPORTANT GEOGRAPHIC CENTRES

II.1. Basel

Basel 1943. *Kunstwerke des 19. Jahrhunderts aus Basler Privatbesitz*, exhibition catalogue, Basel, Kunsthalle, 1943.

G. Oeri, *Kunstwerke des neunzehnten Jahrhunderts aus Basler Privatbesitz*, Basel 1944.

Basel 1945. *Ausländische Kunstwerke des 20. Jahrhunderts aus Basler Privatbesitz*, exhibition catalogue, Basel, Kunsthalle, 1945.

II.2. Bern

Bern 1953. *Europäische Kunst aus Berner Privatbesitz*, exhibition catalogue, Bern, Kunsthalle, 1953 (mainly French Impressionists).

II.3. Winterthur

Winterthur 1911. *Ausstellung von Kunstwerken aus Winterthurer Privatbesitz*, exhibition catalogue, Winterthur, Kunstverein, 1911.

Winterthur 1916. *Ausstellung französischer Malerei im Museum*, exhibition catalogue, Winterthur, Kunstverein, 1916.

H. Bloesch, 'Die Sammlungen im Winterthurer Museum', *Das Werk*, III, 1916, pp. 49–64.

Winterthur 1932. *Verzeichnis der Erwerbungen seit 1913 (1913–1932)*, Winterthur, Galerieverein, 1932.

H. Keller, 'Kunst', *Winterthur, Ein Heimatbuch*, ed. with the support of the municipal council, Winterthur 1935, pp. 135–48.

Winterthur 1942. *Der unbekannte Winterthurer Privatbesitz 1500–1900*, exhibition catalogue, Winterthur, Kunstmuseum/Kunstverein, 1942.

Winterthur 1949. *Winterthurer Privatbesitz II, Werke des 20. Jahrhunderts*, exhibition catalogue, Winterthur, Kunstmuseum/Kunstverein, 1949.

P. Courthion, *Charles Montag, Winterthour, 23 mars 1880–28 juillet 1956* [1956].

Winterthur 1976. *Sammlungskatalog der Gemälde und Plastiken des Kunstvereins*, collection catalogue, Winterthur, Kunstmuseum, 1976.

Winterthur 1980–81. Karl Montag, Winterthur, Kunstmuseum, 1980–81 (an information sheet was published on the occasion of the exhibition).

Winterthur 1990. *Geschichte des Kunstvereins Winterthur seit seiner Gründung 1848*, ed. by the municipal library of Winterthur, 1990.

Winterthur 1991. *Das gloriose Jahrzehnt, Französische Kunst 1910–1920 aus Winterthurer Besitz*, exhibition catalogue, Winterthur, Kunstmuseum, 1991.

Winterthur 1991. *Kunst der Moderne aus der Sammlung des Kunstvereins*, Winterthur, Kunstmuseum, collection catalogue by R. Koella and D. Schwarz, Frankfurt a.M. 1991.

Baden 1992. *Carl Montag, Maler und Kunstvermittler (1880–1956)*, exhibition catalogue by F. Deuchler, Baden, Stiftung 'Langmatt', 1992.

R. Koella, 'A Prime Example of Art Collection in Switzerland' in *Luxe, Calme et Volupté, Regards sur le Post-Impressionnisme, Collectionneurs à Winterthur et Baden au début du XXe siècle*, exhibition catalogue, Luxembourg, Casino, 1995, pp. 57–69.

II.4. Zurich

Zurich 1914. *Aus Zürcher Privatsammlungen*, exhibition catalogue, Zurich, Kunsthaus, 1914 (mainly collection Meyer-Fierz).

Zurich 1927. *Ausstellung von Werken aus dem Besitz von Mitgliedern der Vereinigung Zürcher Kunstfreunde*, exhibition catalogue, Zurich, Kunsthaus, 1927.

P. Ganz, *Zürcher Kunstsinn und Kunstsammeln*, Zurich 1943.

U. Schwarz, *Zürcher Kunstsammler neuester Zeit*, Zurich 1977.

C. Klemm, *Kunsthaus Zürich*, Zurich 1992.

III. PRIVATE COLLECTORS IN SWITZERLAND

III.1. Sidney Brown (1865–1941) and Jenny Brown-Sulzer (1871–1968), Baden, active as collectors as of 1908

P. Courthion, 'La Collection Sidney Brown (= L'Art Français dans les Collections privées en Suisse)', *L'Amour de l'Art*, VII/1, 1926, pp. 27–32.

F. Deuchler, *Die französischen Impressionisten und ihre Vorläufer*, Stiftung 'Langmatt', Sidney und Jenny Brown, Baden, collection catalogue, vol. I, Baden 1990.

F. Deuchler, *Stiftung 'Langmatt', Sidney und Jenny Brown, Baden AG, Karl Mosers Bau, Architektur und Ausstattung*, ed. by Gesellschaft für Schweizerische Kunstgeschichte, Bern 1991.

F. Deuchler, *The 'Langmatt' Foundation, Sidney and Jenny Brown, Baden, A Short Guide to the Painting Collection*, ed. by Gesellschaft für Schweizerische Kunstgeschichte, Bern 1992.

E.-M. Preiswerk-Lösel, 'Winterthur Collectors in Baden: Sidney and Jenny Brown at Villa Langmatt', in *Luxe, Calme et Volupté, Regards sur le Post-Impressionnisme, Collectionneurs à Winterthur et Baden au début du XXe siècle*, exhibition catalogue, Luxembourg, Casino, 1995, pp. 89–95.

III.2. *Richard Bühler (1879–1967), Winterthur, cousin of Hedy Hahnloser-Bühler, president of the Winterthur Kunstverein, active as collector as of c. 1907*

P. Courthion, 'La Collection Bühler (= L'Art Français dans les Collections privées en Suisse)', *L'Amour de l'Art*, VII/2, 1926, pp.59–61.

Bern 1935. *Moderne Graphik aus der Sammlung Richard Bühler, Winterthur*, auction catalogue, Bern, Gutekunst & Klipstein, 1935.

Lucerne 1935. *Sammlung Richard Bühler, Winterthur, Französische Impressionisten, Moderne Schweizer Meister, Zeichnungen, Graphik, Plastik*, auction catalogue, Lucerne, Fischer, 2 September 1935.

Paris 1937. *Tableaux Modernes provenant de la collection de Monsieur R. B…*, auction catalogue, Paris, Drouot, 3 June 1937.

K. Medici-Mall, *Das Landhaus Waldbühl von H.M. Baillie Scott, Ein Gesamtkunstwerk zwischen Neugotik und Jugendstil*, Bern 1979.

III.3. *Emil Georg Bührle (1890–1956), Zurich, active as collector as of 1934*

R. Wehrli, 'Emil G. Bührle', in *Great Private Collections*, ed. by D. Cooper and K. Clark, London 1963, pp.216–27.

Zurich and Munich 1973, *Stiftung Sammlung Emil G. Bührle*, collection catalogue, Zurich and Munich 1973.

E. Maurer, *Stiftung Sammlung E.G. Bührle, Zürich*, collection brochure, ed. by Gesellschaft für Schweizerische Kunstgeschichte, Bern 1992.

Washington et al. 1990–91. *The Passionate Eye/Un regard passionné*, exhibition catalogue on the occasion of the 100th anniversary of the collector Emil G. Bührle, Washington, National Gallery of Art, et al., 1990–91.

III.4. *Arthur Hahnloser (1870–1936) and Hedy Hahnloser-Bühler (1873–1952), Winterthur, active as collectors as of 1907*

H. Hahnloser-Bühler, 'Vorbilder der schweizerischen Kunst' (response to an article by Ernst Würtenberger), *Nationalzeitung* (Basel), no.364, 18 August 1919, unpaginated.

H. Hahnloser-Bühler, 'Kunstpflege in der Schweiz', *Nationalzeitung* (Basel), special issue 'Schweizer Kunst', with no.431, 26 September 1919.

P. Courthion, 'La Collection Arthur Hahnloser (= L'Art Français dans les Collections privées en Suisse)', *L'Amour de l'Art*, VII/2, 1926, pp.62–8.

H. Hahnloser-Bühler, 'Um Félix Vallotton, Urteile von Künstlern und Kritikern über Félix Vallotton', *Das Werk*, VIII, 1931, pp.311–15.

Winterthur 1937. *Werke aus der Sammlung Dr. Arthur Hahnloser*, exhibition catalogue, Winterthur, Kunstmuseum, 1937.

H.M. Zeltner and H.R. Hahnloser, 'Private und öffentliche Kunstpflege in Winterthur', *Das ideale Heim*, XI/5, 1937, pp.181–7.

H. Hahnloser-Bühler, 'Les Impressionnistes dans la Collection Hahnloser', foreword of the exhibition catalogue *La Peinture française du XIXᵉ siècle en Suisse*, Paris, Galerie des Beaux-Arts, 1938.

Lucerne 1940. *Die Hauptwerke der Sammlung Hahnloser, Winterthur*, exhibition catalogue, with an introduction by H. Hahnloser-Bühler, Lucerne, Kunstmuseum, 1940.

'Die Sammlung Hahnloser (= Aus Schweizer Privatsammlungen, 3)', *Du, Schweizerische Monatsschrift*, XVI/11, 1956 (special issue devoted to Hahnloser Collection).

Winterthur 1969. *Der Weg ins 20. Jahrhundert, Aus der Entwicklungsgeschichte der modernen Raumkunst in der Schweiz*, exhibition catalogue, Winterthur, Gewerbemuseum, 1969.

Munich 1969. *Europäische Meisterwerke aus Schweizer Sammlungen*, exhibition catalogue, Munich, Staatliche Graphische Sammlung, 1969.

Winterthur 1973. *Künstlerfreunde um Arthur und Hedy Hahnloser-Bühler, Französische und Schweizer Kunst, 1890–1940*, exhibition catalogue, Winterthur, Kunstmuseum, 1973.

M. Hahnloser-Ingold, 'Hodler und seine Freunde in der deutschen Schweiz, Zur Rezeptionsgeschichte um die Jahrhundertwende', in *Hodler und Freiburg, Die Mission des Künstlers*, exhibition catalogue, Freiburg, Museum für Kunst und Geschichte, 1981, pp.63–87.

M. Hahnloser-Ingold, 'History of the Collection at the Villa Flora', in *Luxe, Calme et Volupté, Regards sur le Post-Impressionnisme, Collectionneurs à Winterthur et Baden au début du XXᵉ siècle*, exhibition catalogue, Luxembourg, Casino, 1995, pp.71–83.

III.5. *Emil Hahnloser (1874–1940), Winterthur, brother-in-law of Hedy Hahnloser-Bühler*

P. Courthion, 'La Collection Emile Hahnloser (= L'Art Français dans les Collections privées en Suisse)', *L'Amour de l'Art*, VII/2, 1926, pp.50–6.

III.6. *Gustav Henneberg (1847–1918), Zurich, art dealer, first collection before 1895–1903 (sold by auction in Munich), second collection as of 1908; the collection was sold by auction after his death*

Zurich 1911. *Galerie Henneberg*, collection catalogue, Zurich 1911.

Zurich 1919. *Sammlung G. Henneberg, Zürich, Ölgemälde und Zeichnungen hervorragender Meister des XIX. Jahrhunderts (Kunstgegenstände)*, auction catalogue, Zurich, Neupert/Messikommer, 20–25 October 1919.

III.7. *Richard Kisling (1862–1917), Zurich, member of the exhibition commission of the Zürcher Kunstgesellschaft, active as collector as of 1902; the collection was sold by auction after his death*

Zurich 1913. *Eine Zürcher Privat-Sammlung, Schweizer Kunst des 19. und 20. Jahrhunderts*, exhibition catalogue, Zurich, Kunsthaus, 1913.

H. Bloesch, 'Das Heim eines Mäzens', *Das Werk*, V, 1918, pp.101–9.

W. Wartmann, *Richard Kisling, ein Kunstfreund, 1862–1917*, Zurich, n.d.

H. Ganz, 'Die Sammlung Kisling in Zürich', *Das Werk*, XVI, 1929, pp.316–19.

Zurich 1929. *Sammlung Richard Kisling (u.a. anderem Besitz)*, auction catalogue, Zurich, G. & L. Bollag, 18 November 1929.

V. Ehrli, *Der moderne Bund, Wilhelm Wartmann und Richard Kisling*, master's thesis, Zurich 1981, Ms.

III.8. *Hans Mettler (1876–1945), St Gallen, distant relative of Bühler family, Winterthur, active as collector as of 1915*

London 1979. *The Collection of Impressionist and Post-Impressionist Paintings, formed by The late Mr. Hans Mettler of St. Gallen, Switzerland*, auction catalogue, London, Christie's, 2 July 1979.

III.9. *Fritz Meyer-Fierz (1847–1917), Zurich, active as collector as of c. 1880*

Zurich 1914. *Aus Zürcher Privatsammlungen*, exhibition catalogue, Zurich, Kunsthaus, 1914.

Amsterdam 1926. *Collection Fritz Meyer de Zurich, Tableaux modernes, aquarelles*, auction catalogue, Amsterdam, Muller & Cie, 13 July 1926.

III.10. Oscar Miller (1862–1934), Biberist (Solothurn), active as collector as of 1896; collected mainly Swiss modern art

O. Miller, *Von Stoff zu Form*, Frauenfeld 1904 (extended editions ²1906 and 1907, ³1913).

O. Miller, *Das Grundprinzip der Kunst*, Frauenfeld 1905.

O. Miller, 'Mein Verhältnis zur heutigen Malerei', *Wissen und Leben*, III, 1908/09, pp.460–73.

O. Miller, '"L'art pour l'art"', *Wissen und Leben*, IV, 1909/10, pp.228–30.

W. Reitz, 'Die Kunstsammlung Oscar Miller, Biberist', *Wissen und Leben*, XIV/15, 1920/21, pp.726–31.

Bern 1921. *Sammlung Oscar Miller, Biberist*, exhibition catalogue, Bern, Kunsthalle, 1921.

III.11. Josef Müller (1887–1977) and Gertrud Dübi-Müller (1888–1980), Solothurn, active as collectors as of 1907/08

Solothurn 1950. *Hundert Jahre Malerei aus Solothurner Privatbesitz*, exhibition catalogue, Solothurn, Museum der Stadt, 1950.

Solothurn 1975. *Schweizer Kunst in der Sammlung Josef Müller*, exhibition catalogue, Solothurn, Museum der Stadt, 1975.

G. Germann, *Regesten zu den Akten Dübi-Müller, Solothurn*, Zurich 1981, Ms.

Solothurn 1981. *Dübi-Müller-Stiftung, Josef Müller-Stiftung*, exhibition catalogue, Solothurn, Kunstmuseum, 1981.

J.P. and M. Barbier-Mueller, ed., *Aus dem Leben eines Sammlers, Josef Müller, 1887–1977*, Milan 1989.

III.12. Georg Reinhart, 1877–1955, Winterthur, son of Theodor Reinhart, brother of Oskar Reinhart, active as collector as of 1904, collecting Impressionist painting as of 1911

G. Reinhart, *Katalog meiner Sammlung*, collection catalogue, Winterthur 1922.

P. Courthion, 'La Collection Georges Reinhart (= L'Art Français dans les Collections privées en Suisse)', *L'Amour de l'Art*, VII/2, 1926, pp.47–9.

G. Reinhart, *Aus meinem Leben*, Winterthur 1931.

III.13. Oskar Reinhart (1885–1965), Winterthur, active as collector as of 1913; donated his collection to the Swiss Confederation

P. Courthion, 'La Collection Oscar Reinhart (= L'Art Français dans les Collections privées en Suisse)', *L'Amour de l'Art*, VII/1, 1926, pp.3–26.

K. Scheffler, 'Die Sammlung Oskar Reinhart in Winterthur', *Kunst und Künstler*, XXV, 1926/27, pp.3–13.

W. George, 'Collection Oskar Reinhart, Topographie d'une collection', *Formes*, nos.26/27, 1932.

J. Meier-Graefe, 'Die Sammlung Oskar Reinhart', *Frankfurter Zeitung*, 29 April/12 May 1932.

R. Seiffert-Wattenberg, *Aus der Sammlung Oskar Reinhart*, Munich [1935].

L. Vitali, 'Le grandi collezioni, I: La raccolta Oskar Reinhart a Winterthur', *Emporium*, no.43, 1937, pp.59ff.

Bern 1939–40. *Sammlung Oskar Reinhart Winterthur*, exhibition catalogue, Bern, Kunstmuseum, 1939–40.

A. Huth, 'A Swiss Collection of Masterpieces exhibited at the Berne Museum', *The Studio*, no.119, 1940, pp.194ff.

P. Budry, 'La collection Reinhart et la peinture française', *Formes et Couleurs*, nos.2/3, 1940, unpaginated.

Meisterwerke europäischer Malerei des XV.–XIX. Jahrhunderts aus der Sammlung Oskar Reinhart, (4 portfolios of plates), ed. by H. Zbinden, Bern 1940–41.

Zurich 1940–41. *Sammlung Oskar Reinhart, Alte Meister und französische Maler des 19. Jahrhunderts*, with an introduction by W. Wartmann, exhibition catalogue, Zurich, Kunsthaus, 1940–41.

G. Jedlicka, 'Die Sammlung Oskar Reinhart', *Frankfurter Zeitung*, nos.244/5, 14–15 May 1941.

G. Jedlicka, 'Oskar Reinhart, Zu seinem sechzigsten Geburtstag, 11. Juni 1945', *Das Werk*, XXXII, 1945, pp.161ff.

F. Daulte, 'Depuis plus de trente ans, Oscar Reinhart collectionne des tableaux pour former un musée de chefs-d'œuvre qu'il léguera à la Suisse', *Connaissance des Arts*, no.26, 1954, pp.22ff.

'Die Privatsammlung Oskar Reinhart (= Aus Schweizer Privatsammlungen, 2)', *Du, Schweizerische Monatsschrift*, XVI/8, 1956 (special issue devoted to Oskar Reinhart Collection).

D. Cooper, 'Oskar Reinhart', in *Great Private Collections*, ed. by D. Cooper and K. Clark, London 1963, pp.204–15.

Sammlung Oskar Reinhart, Am Römerholz, collection handbook, ed. by the Swiss Confederation, with an introduction by L. Stähelin, Winterthur [1970].

R. Koella, *Sammlungskatalog Oskar Reinhart, Am Römerholz, Winterthur, Bilder, Zeichnungen, Plastiken*, collection catalogue, Zurich 1975.

R. Koella, *Sammlung Oskar Reinhart Am Römerholz, Winterthur*, collection broschure, ed. by Gesellschaft für Schweizerische Kunstgeschichte, Basel 1975.

III.14. Theodor Reinhart (1849–1919), Winterthur

W. Hugelshofer, ed., *Der Briefwechsel zwischen Dr. Theodor Reinhart und Robert Zünd*, Winterthur 1940.

III.15. Hans Schuler (1869–1920), Zurich, cousin of Hedy Hahnloser-Bühler, member of the collecting commission of the Zürcher Kunstgesellschaft, active as collector as of 1906; the collection was bequeathed to the Kunsthaus Zurich

H. Schuler, 'Impressionismus, Eine Entgegnung', *Wissen und Leben*, II, 1908/09, pp.292–9.

III.16. Rudolf Staechelin (1881–1946), Basel, active as collector as of c.1914

Basel 1920. *September-Ausstellung (Gemälde aus Privatbesitz)*, exhibition catalogue, Basel, Kunsthalle, 1920.

Basel 1956. *Sammlung Rudolf Staechelin*, exhibition on the occasion of the 10th anniversary of the collector's death, exhibition catalogue, Basel, Kunstmuseum, 1956.

H.-J. Müller, *Nafea, The Rudolf Staechelin Collection Basel/Nafea, La Collezione Rudolf Staechelin Basilea*, with essays by C. Geelhaar, F. Meyer, S. de Pury, R. Staechelin, Basel 1991.

III.17. Emil Staub (1867–1929), Männedorf

P. Courthion, 'La Collection Emile Staub (= L'Art Français dans les Collections privées en Suisse)', *L'Amour de l'Art*, VII/2, 1926, pp.37–46.

W. George, 'La collection Staub à Männedorf', *Formes*, XXV, 1932, pp.271ff.

III.18. Arthur Stoll (1887–1971), Arlesheim (BL), active as collector as of c.1934

Katalog der Sammlung Arthur Stoll, Skulpturen und Gemälde des 19. und 20. Jahrhunderts, with an introduction by M. Fischer, ed. by Schweizerisches Institut für Kunstwissenschaft, Zurich and Stuttgart 1961.

Bern 1972. *Kunstwerke aus der Sammlung Stoll*, auction catalogue, Bern, Kornfeld & Klipstein, 18 November 1972 (auction no.146).

INDEX

PHOTOGRAPHIC CREDITS

FRIENDS OF THE ROYAL ACADEMY

SPONSORS

Mrs Denise Adeane
Mr P.F.J. Bennett
Mrs D. Berger
Mr David Berman
Mrs J. Brice
Mr Jeremy Brown
Mrs L. Cantor
The Caroll Foundation
Mr and Mrs Christopher Cates
Mrs Elizabeth Corob
Mr and Mrs S. Fein
Mr M.J. Fitzgerald (Occidental
    International Oil Inc.)
Mr and Mrs R. Gapper
Mr and Mrs Robert Gavron
Mr and Mrs Michael Godbee
Lady Gosling
Mr Peter G. Goulandris
Lady Grant
Mr Harold Joels
Mrs G. Jungels-Winkler
Mr J. Kirkman
Dr Abraham Marcus
The Oakmoor Trust
Ocean Group p.l.c. (P.H. Holt Trust)
The Worshipful Company of Saddlers
Mr and Mrs David Shalit
The Stanley Foundation
Mrs Paula Swift
Mr Robin Symes
Mrs Edna S. Weiss
Sir Brian Wolfson

ASSOCIATE SPONSORS

Mr Richard B. Allan
Mrs Meg Allen
Mr Richard Alston
Mr Ian F.C. Anstruther
Mrs Ann Appelbe
Mr John R. Asprey
Lady Attenborough
Mr J.M. Bartos
Mr N.S. Bergel
Mrs J.L. Berger

Mrs Susan Besser
Mrs Linda Blackstone
Mrs C.W.T. Blackwell
Mr Peter Boizot
C.T. Bowring (Charities Trust) Ltd
Mrs J.M. Bracegirdle
Mr Cornelius Broere
Lady Brown
Mr P.J. Brown Jr
Mrs Susan Burns
Mrs A. Cadbury
Mr and Mrs P.H.G. Cadbury
Mr and Mrs R. Cadbury
Mrs C.A. Cain
Miss E.M. Cassin
Mr R.A. Cernis
Mr S. Chapman
Mr W.J. Chapman
Mr. M. Chowen
Mrs J.V. Clarke
Mr John Cleese
Mrs D. Cohen
Mrs R. Cohen
Mrs N.S. Conrad
Mr C. Cotton
Mrs Saeda H. Dalloul
Mr and Mrs D. de Laszlo
Mr John Denham
Mr Richard Dobson
The Marquess of Douro
Mr D.P. Duncan
Mr J. Edwards
Mr Kenneth Edwards
Mrs K.W. Feesey MSc
Mrs B.D. Fenton
Mr J.G. Fogel
Mr Graham Gauld
Mr Stephen A. Geiger
Mrs P. Goldsmith
Mr Gavin Graham
Mrs O. Grogan
Mr J.A. Hadjipateras
Mr B.R.H. Hall
Mr and Mrs D. Hallam-Peel
Mr and Mrs Richard Harris
Miss Julia Hazandras
Mr M.Z. Hepker
Mr Malcolm Herring

Mrs P. Heseltine
Mrs K.S. Hill
Mr R.J. Hoare
Mr Reginald Hoe
Mr Charles Howard
Mrs A. Howitt
Mr Christopher Hull
Mr Norman J. Hyams
Mr David Hyman
Mrs Manya Igel
Mr C.J. Ingram
Mr S. Isern-Feliu
The Rt. Hon. The Countess of Iveagh
Mrs I. Jackson
Lady Jacobs
Mrs G. Jungels-Winkler
Mr and Mrs S.D. Kahan
Mr Simon Karmel
Mr D.H. Killick
Mr P.W. Kininmonth
Mrs L. Kosta
Mrs. E. Landau
Mr and Mrs M.J. Langer
Mrs J.H. Lavender
Mr Morris Leigh
Mr Owen Luder
Mrs G.M.S. McIntosh
Mr Peter I. McMean
The Hon. Simon Marks
Mr and Mrs V.J. Marmion
Mr B.P. Marsh
Mr and Mrs J.B.H. Martin
Mr R.C. Martin
Mrs Catherine Martineau
Mr and Mrs G. Mathieson
Mr. R. Matthews
Mr J. Menasakanian
Mr J. Moores
Mrs A. Morgan
Mrs A. Morrison
Mr A.H.J. Muir
Mr David H. Nelson
Mrs E.M. Oppenheim-Sandelson
Mr Brian R. Oury
Mrs J. Palmer
Mr J.H. Pattisson
Mrs M.C.S. Philip
Mrs Anne Phillips

Mr Ralph Picken
Mr G.B. Pincus
Mr G.A. Pitt-Rivers
Mr W. Plapinger
Mrs J. Rich
Mr Clive and Mrs Sylvia Richards
Mr F.P. Robinson
Mr D. Rocklin
Mrs A. Rodman
Lady Rootes
Mr and Mrs O. Roux
The Hon. Sir Stephen Runciman CH
Sir Robert Sainsbury
Mr G. Salmanowitz
Lady Samuel
Mrs Bernice Sandelson
Mrs Bernard L. Schwartz
Mr M. Sheldon
Shell UK Ltd
Mr Mark Shelmerdine
Mr R.J. Simmons
Mr John H.M. Sims
Mr and Mrs M.L. Slotover
Mr and Mrs R. Slotover
The Spencer Wills Trust
Mrs B. Stubbs
Mr J.A. Tackaberry
Mr and Mrs L. Tanner
Mr N. Tarling
Mr G.C.A. Thom
Mr H.R. Towning
Mrs Andrew Trollope
Mr E. Victor
Mr A.J. Vines
Mrs C.H. Walton
Mr D.R. Walton Masters
Mr Neil Warren
Miss J. Waterous
Mrs J.M. Weingarten
Mrs C. Weldon
Mr Frank S. Wenstrom
Mr J. Wickham
Mrs I. Wolstenholme
Mr W.M. Wood
Mr R.M. Woodhouse
Mr F.S. Worms

ROYAL ACADEMY TRUST

BENEFACTORS

H.M. The Queen
Mr and Mrs Russell B. Aitken
American Airlines
The Annie Laurie Aitkin Charitable Trust
American Associates of the Royal Academy Trust
American Express Company
Mrs John W. Anderson II

The Andor Family
The Hon. and Mrs Walter H. Annenberg
Mr Walter Archibald
Marilyn B. Arison
The Hon. Anne and Mr Tobin Armstrong
Asprey
AT & T
AT & T (UK) Ltd
The Bank of England

Barclays Bank plc
The Baring Foundation
B.A.T. Industries plc
Mr Tom Bendhem
Benihana Group
Mr and Mrs James Benson
Mrs Brenda Benwell-Lejeune
In Memoriam: Ida Rose Biggs
Charlotte Bonham-Carter Charitable Trust

Bowne of New York City
Mr Peter Bowring
British Airways, North America
British Gas plc
The British Petroleum Company plc
BP America
British Steel plc
Mr Keith Bromley
The Brown Foundation Inc.

BT
Bunzl plc
Iris and B. Gerald Cantor
The Rt. Hon. the Lord Carrington
The Trustees of the Clore Foundation
The John S. Cohen Foundation
The Cohen Family Charitable Trust
The Colby Trust
Commercial Union Assurance Company PLC
The Ernest Cook Trust
Mrs Jan Cowles
Crabtree & Evelyn
Credit Suisse First Boston
The Hon. and Mrs C. Douglas Dillon
Sir Harry and Lady Djanogly
In Memoriam: Miss W.A. Donner
Alfred Dunhill Limited
Miss Jayne Edwardes
The John Ellerman Foundation
English Heritage
Esso UK PLC
The Esmée Fairbairn Charitable Trust
Lord and Lady Faringdon
Mr and Mrs Eugene V. Fife
Mr and Mrs Donald R. Findlay
Mr D. Francis Finlay
The Hon. and Mrs Leonard K. Firestone
Mr Walter Fitch III
Mrs Henry Ford II
The Henry Ford II Fund
The Late John Frye Bourne
The Garfield Weston Foundation
The Gatsby Foundation
The Getty Grant Program
The J. Paul Getty Jr Trust
The Lady Gibson
Glaxo
Mrs Mary Graves
The Jack Goldhill Charitable Trust
The Horace W. Goldsmith Foundation
The Worshipful Company of Goldsmiths
Mr and Mrs John Gore
The Gosling Foundation Ltd
The Greentree Foundation
Mr Lewis Grinnan Jr
The Worshipful Company of Grocers
The Worshipful Company of Haberdashers
The Paul Hamlyn Foundation
The Late Dr and Mrs Armand Hammer
Mrs Sue Hammerson
Philip and Pauline Harris Charitable Trust
The Hayward Foundation
The Hawser Foundation
Mr and Mrs Randolph Hearst
The Hedley Foundation
Mrs Henry J. Heinz
The Henry J. and Drue Heinz Foundation
The Drue Heinz Trust
The Heritage of London Trust
IBM United Kingdom Limited
The Idlewild Trust
The Inchcape Charitable Trust
The Worshipful Company of Ironmongers
Mr and Mrs Ralph Isham
The J.P. Jacobs Charitable Trust
Jerwood Foundation
Mr and Mrs Donald P. Kahn
Mrs D. King
KPMG Peat Marwick

Irene and Hyman Kreitman
The Kresge Foundation
The Kress Foundation
Mr and Mrs Sol Kroll
Ladbroke Group Plc
Mr D.E. Laing
The Maurice Laing Foundation
The Landmark Trust
Mr John S. Latsis
The Leche Trust
The Leverhulme Trust
Mr Leon Levy and Ms Shelby White
Mr J.H. Lewis
Lex Services PLC
The Linbury Trust
The Ruth and Stuart Lipton Charitable Trust
Sir Sydney and Lady Lipworth
Lloyds Bank PLC
Mr John Madejski
Mrs T.S. Mallinson
The Manifold Trust
The Stella and Alexander Margulies
    Charitable Trust
Mr and Mrs John L. Marion
Mrs W. Marks
Marks & Spencer
Mrs Jack C. Massey
M. J. Meehan & Company
Paul Mellon KBE
The Anthony and Elizabeth Mellows
    Charitable Trust
The Mercers' Company
The Henry Moore Foundation
Museums and Galleries Improvement Fund
National Westminster Bank PLC
Mr Stavros S. Niarchos
Ms Diane A. Nixon
Orrin Charitable Trust
Otemae College
The Peacock Charitable Trust
Mr and Mrs Frank Pearl
The Pennycress Trust
In Memoriam: Mrs Olive Petit
Mr and Mrs Milton Petrie
The P.F. Charitable Trust
The Pilgrim Trust
Mr A.N. Polhill
The Hon. and Mrs Leon B. Polsky
The Hon. and Mrs Charles H. Price II
Prudential Assurance Company Ltd
The Radcliffe Trust
The Rayne Foundation
The Regent Hotel
Mr and Mrs Laurance S. Rockefeller
The Ronson Charitable Foundation
The J. Rothschild Group Charitable Trust
Rothschilds Inc
The RTZ Corporation Plc
The Late Dr Arthur M. Sackler
Mrs Arthur M. Sackler
The Sainsbury Family Charitable Trusts
Mrs Jean Sainsbury
Mrs Basil Samuel
Mrs Louisa Sarofim
Save & Prosper Educational Trust
Sea Containers Limited
Shell UK Ltd
The Archie Sherman Charitable Trust
Mr and Mrs James C. Slaughter

The Late Mr Robert Slaughter
Pauline Denyer Smith and Paul Smith CBE
The Spencer Charitable Trust
Miss K. Stalnaker
Mr and Mrs Stephen Stamas
The Starr Foundation
Mr and Mrs Robert K. Steel
Bernard Sunley Charitable Foundation
John Swire and Son
Mr and Mrs A. Alfred Taubman
Mr and Mrs Vernon Taylor Jr.
Texaco Inc
G. Ware and Edythe Travelstead
The TSB Foundation for England and Wales
Seiji Tsutsumi
The Douglas Turner Charitable Trust
The 20th May 1961 Charitable Trust
Unilever PLC
Mr Alexander Von Auersperg
The Henry Vyner Charitable Trust
S.G. Warburg Limited
Dorothy, Viscountess Weir
The Weldon UK Charitable Trust
Mr and Mrs Keith S. Wellin
The Welton Foundation
Westminster City Council
Mr and Mrs Garry H. Weston
Mr Anthony Whishaw RA
Mr Frederick B. Whittemore
The Hon. and Mrs John Whitehead
Mrs John Hay Whitney
Mr and Mrs Wallace S. Wilson
Mr A. Witkin
The Wolfson Foundation
The Late Mr Charles Wollaston
The Late Mr Ian Woodner
Mr and Mrs William Wood Prince

CORPORATE MEMBERS

Arthur Andersen & Andersen Consulting
Ashurst Morris Crisp
Atlantic Plastics Limited
A.T. Kearney Limited
Bankers Trust
Banque Indosuez
Barclays de Zoete Wedd
BAT Industries plc
BP Chemicals
British Aerospace plc
British Alcan Aluminium plc
British Gas plc
British Petroleum
BT
Bunzl plc
Capital International Ltd
Christie's
Chubb Insurance Company
Cookson Group plc
Coopers & Lybrand
Courage Limited
C.S. First Boston Group
The Daily Telegraph plc
Datastream International
Department of National Heritage
The Diamond Trading Company (Pty) Limited
DuPont (U.K.) Ltd.
French Railways Ltd.

Gartmore plc
Goldman Sachs International Limited
Glaxo Holdings p.l.c.
Grand Metropolitan plc
Guinness PLC
Hay Management Consultants Ltd
Hill Samuel Bank Limited
Hillier Parker May & Rowden
ICI
Industrial Bank of Japan, Limited
Jaguar Cars Ltd
John Laing plc
Lehman Brothers International
Lloyds Private Banking Limited
London & Edinburgh Trust plc
E.D.& F. Man Limited Charitable Trust
Marks & Spencer
Merrill Lynch Europe Ltd
McKinsey's
Midland Group
MoMart plc
J.P. Morgan
Morgan Stanley International
Newton Investment Management Limited
The Peninsular and Oriental Steam Navigation Co
The Reader's Digest Association
Republic National Bank of New York
Reuters
Rothmans International p.l.c.
Rothmans International Tobacco (UK) Ltd
Royal Bank of Scotland plc
The RTZ Corporation PLC
Salomon Brothers
Santa Fe Exploration (U.K.) Limited
Sea Containers Ltd.
Silhouette Eyewear
SmithKline Beecham
Smith & Williamson
Société Générale
Société Générale de Belgique
Southern Water plc
TI Group plc
Tractebel
Trafalgar House Construction Holdings Ltd
Unilever PLC
Union Minière
Visa International Europe, Middle East,
    Africa Region

CORPORATE ASSOCIATES

A T & T
Bass PLC
BMP DDB Needham
BMW (GB) Ltd
The BOC Group
Booker plc
Bovis Construction Ltd
Cable and Wireless plc
Charterhouse plc
CJA (Management Recruitment Consultants)
    Limited
Clifford Chance
Coutts & Co
Credit Lyonnais Laing
The Dai-Ichi Kangyo Bank Limited
Dalgleish & Co
De La Rue plc

Durrington Corporation Limited
Enterprise Oil plc
Fina plc
Foreign & Colonial Management Ltd
Forte plc
General Accident plc
The General Electric Company plc
Guardian Royal Exchange plc
Hamilton Oil Company Ltd
Heidrick & Struggles Int.
H.J. Heinz Company Limited
IBM UK Ltd
Inchcape plc
S.C. Johnson

Kleinwort Benson Limited
Kodak Limited
Lex Service PLC
Linklaters and Paines
John Lewis Partnership plc
Lloyds Bank plc
Macfarlanes
Mars G.B. Limited
Nabarro Nathanson
Nat West Investment Management
NEC (UK) Ltd
Northern Telecom Europe Ltd
Occidental International Oil Inc
Olivetti UK Limited

Ove Arup Partnership
Pearson plc
Pentland Group plc
The Post Office
The Rank Organisation Plc
Reliance National Insurance Company (UK) Ltd
Robert Fleming & Co Limited
Royal Insurance Holdings plc
Sainsbury's PLC
Save & Prosper Educational Trust
Schroder Investment Management Ltd
J. Henry Schroder Wagg & Co Limited
Sears plc
Sedgwick Group plc

Slough Estates plc
Smith Systems Engineering
Sony United Kingdom Limited
Sotheby's
Sun Life Assurance Society plc
Tate & Lyle Plc
Tomkins PLC
Toyota Motor Corporation
United Biscuits (UK) Ltd
Vistech International Ltd
The Wellcome Foundation Ltd

SPONSORS OF PAST EXHIBITIONS

The Council of the Royal Academy thanks sponsors of past exhibitions for their support.
Sponsors of major exhibitions during the last ten years have included the following:

ALITALIA
Italian Art in the 20th Century 1989

AMERICAN EXPRESS FOUNDATION
Je suis le cahier: The Sketchbooks of Picasso 1986

ARTS COUNCIL OF GREAT BRITAIN
Peter Greenham 1985

THE BANQUE INDOSUEZ GROUP
Pissarro: The Impressionist and the City 1993

BANQUE INDOSUEZ AND W.I. CARR
Gauguin and The School of Pont-Aven:
   Prints and Paintings 1989

BBC RADIO ONE
The Pop Art Show 1991

BECK'S BIER
German Art in the 20th Century 1985

BMW 8 SERIES
Georges Rouault: The Early Years, 1903–1920
   1993

ROBERT BOSCH LIMITED
German Art in the 20th Century 1985

BOVIS CONSTRUCTION LTD
New Architecture 1986

BRITISH ALCAN ALUMINIUM
Sir Alfred Gilbert 1986

BRITISH PETROLEUM PLC
British Art in the 20th Century 1987

BT
Hokusai 1991

CANARY WHARF DEVELOPMENT
New Architecture 1986

THE CAPITAL GROUP COMPANIES
Drawings from the J. Paul Getty Museum 1993

THE CHASE MANHATTAN BANK
Cézanne: the Early Years 1988

CLASSIC FM
Goya: Truth and Fantasy, The Small Paintings 1994

The Glory of Venice: Art in the Eighteenth Century
   1994

THE DAI-ICHI KANGYO BANK LIMITED
222nd Summer Exhibition 1990

THE DAILY TELEGRAPH
American Art in the 20th Century 1993

DEUTSCHE BANK AG
German Art in the 20th Century 1985

DIGITAL EQUIPMENT CORPORATION
Monet in the '90s: The Series Paintings 1990

THE DRUE HEINZ TRUST
The Palladian Revival: Lord Burlington and his
   house and garden at Chiswick

THE DUPONT COMPANY
American Art in the 20th Century 1993

THE ECONOMIST
Inigo Jones Architect 1989

EDWARDIAN HOTELS
The Edwardians and After: Paintings and
   Sculpture from the Royal Academy's Collection,
   1900–1950 1990

ELECTRICITY COUNCIL
New Architecture 1986

ELF
Alfred Sisley 1992

ESSO PETROLEUM COMPANY LTD
220th Summer Exhibition 1988

FIAT
Italian Art in the 20th Century 1989

FINANCIAL TIMES
Inigo Jones Architect 1989

FIRST NATIONAL BANK OF CHICAGO
Chagall 1985

FONDATION ELF
Alfred Sisley 1992

FORD MOTOR COMPANY LIMITED
The Fauve Landscape: Matisse, Derain, Braque
   and their Circle 1991

FRIENDS OF THE ROYAL ACADEMY
Peter Greenham 1985
Sir Alfred Gilbert 1986

GAMLESTADEN
Royal Treasures of Sweden, 1550–1700 1989

JOSEPH GARTNER
New Architecture 1986

J. PAUL GETTY JR CHARITABLE TRUST
The Age of Chivalry 1987

GLAXO HOLDINGS PLC
From Byzantium to El Greco 1987
Great Impressionist and other Master Paintings
   from the Emil G. Bührle Collection, Zurich
   1991
The Unknown Modigliani 1994

THE GUARDIAN
The Unknown Modigliani 1994

GUINNESS PLC
Twentieth-Century Modern Masters: The Jacques
   and Natasha Gelman Collection 1990
223rd Summer Exhibition 1991
224th Summer Exhibition 1992
225th Summer Exhibition 1993
226th Summer Exhibition 1994

GUINNESS PEAT AVIATION
Alexander Calder 1992

HARPERS & QUEEN
Georges Rouault: The Early Years, 1903–1920
   1993
Sandra Blow 1994

THE HENRY MOORE FOUNDATION
Henry Moore 1988
Alexander Calder 1992

HOECHST (UK) LTD
German Art in the 20th Century 1985

THE INDEPENDENT
The Art of Photography 1839–1989 1989
The Pop Art Show 1991

THE INDUSTRIAL BANK OF JAPAN
Hokusai 1991

INTERCRAFT DESIGNS LIMITED
Inigo Jones Architect 1989

JOANNOU & PARASKE-VAIDES
(OVERSEAS) LTD
From Byzantium to El Greco 1987

THE KLEINWORT BENSON GROUP
Inigo Jones Architect 1989

LLOYDS BANK
The Age of Chivalry 1987

LOGICA
The Art of Photography, 1839–1989 1989

LUFTHANSA
German Art in the 20th Century 1985

THE MAIL ON SUNDAY
Royal Academy Summer Season 1992
Royal Academy Summer Season 1993

MARTINI & ROSSI LTD
The Great Age of British Watercolours,
   1750–1880 1993

MARKS & SPENCER PLC
Royal Academy Schools Premiums 1994
Royal Academy Schools Final Year Show 1994

MELITTA
German Art in the 20th Century 1985

PAUL MELLON KBE
The Great Age of British Watercolours,
   1750–1880 1993

MERCEDES-BENZ
German Art in the 20th Century 1985

MERCURY COMMUNICATIONS
The Pop Art Show 1991

MERRILL LYNCH
American Art in the 20th Century 1993

MIDLAND BANK PLC
The Art of Photography 1839–1989 1989
RA Outreach Programme 1992–1995
Lessons in Life 1994

MITSUBISHI ESTATE COMPANY UK
LIMITED
Sir Christopher Wren and the Making of St Paul's 1991

MOBIL
From Byzantium to El Greco 1987

NATIONAL WESTMINSTER BANK
Reynolds 1986
Nicolas Poussin 1594–1665, 1995

OLIVETTI
Andrea Mantegna 1992

OTIS ELEVATORS
New Architecture 1986

PARK TOWER REALTY
CORPORATION
Sir Christopher Wren and the Making of St Paul's 1991

PEARSON PLC
Eduardo Paolozzi Underground 1986

PILKINGTON GLASS
New Architecture 1986

REDAB (UK) LTD
Wisdom and Compassion: The Sacred Art of Tibet 1992

REED INTERNATIONAL PLC
Toulouse-Lautrec: The Graphic Works 1988
Sir Christopher Wren and the Making of St Paul's 1991

REPUBLIC NATIONAL BANK
OF NEW YORK
Sickert: Paintings 1992

ARTHUR M. SACKLER FOUNDATION
Jewels of the Ancients 1987

SALOMON BROTHERS
Henry Moore 1988

THE SARA LEE FOUNDATION
Odilon Redon: Dreams and Visions 1995

SIEMENS
German Art in the 20th Century 1985

SEA CONTAINERS LTD
The Glory of Venice: Art in the Eighteenth Century 1994

SILHOUETTE EYEWEAR
Egon Schiele and His Contemporaries: From the Leopold Collection, Vienna 1990
Wisdom and Compassion: The Sacred Art of Tibet 1992
Sandra Blow 1994

SOCIÉTÉ GÉNÉRALE DE BELGIQUE
Impressionism to Symbolism: The Belgian Avant-Garde 1880–1900 1994

SPERO COMMUNICATIONS
The Schools Final Year Show 1992

SWAN HELLENIC
Edward Lear 1985

TEXACO
Selections from the Royal Academy's Private Collection 1991

THE TIMES
Old Master Paintings from the Thyssen-Bornemisza Collection 1988
Wisdom and Compassion: The Sacred Art of Tibet 1992

Drawings from the J. Paul Getty Museum 1993
Goya: Truth and Fantasy, The Small Paintings 1994

TRACTEBEL
Impressionism to Symbolism: The Belgian Avant-Garde 1880–1900 1994

TRAFALGAR HOUSE
Elisabeth Frink 1985

TRUSTHOUSE FORTE
Edward Lear 1985

UNILEVER
Frans Hals 1990

UNION MINIÈRE
Impressionism to Symbolism: The Belgian Avant-Garde 1880–1900 1994

VISTECH INTERNATIONAL LTD
Wisdom and Compassion: The Sacred Art of Tibet 1992

WALKER BOOKS LIMITED
Edward Lear 1985

OTHER SPONSORS

Sponsors of events, publications and other items in the past two years:

Academy Group Limited
Air Namibia
Air Seychelles
Air UK
Alitalia
American Airlines
Arthur Andersen
Athenaeum Hotel and Apartments
Austrian Airlines
Berggruen & Zevi Limited
British Airways
British Mediterranean Airways
British Midland
Bulgari Jewellery
Cable & Wireless
Christies International plc
Citibank N.A.

Columbus Communications
Condé Nast Publications
Brenda Evans
Fina Plc
Forte Plc
The Four Seasons Hotels
Ghana Airways Corporation
Häagen-Dazs
Tim Harvey Design
Hyundai Car (UK) Ltd
IBM United Kingdom Limited
Inter-Continental Hotels
Intercraft Designs Limited
Jaguar Cars Limited
John Lewis Partnership plc
A.T. Kearney Limited
KLM

The Leading Hotels of the World
Magic of Italy
Martini & Rossi Ltd
May Fair Inter-Continental Hotels
Mercury Communications Ltd
Merrill Lynch
Midland Bank Plc
Anton Mosimann
NK
Novell U.K. Ltd
Patagonia
Penshurst Press Ltd
Percy Fox and Co
Polaroid (UK) Ltd
The Regent Hotel
The Robina Group
Royal Mail International

Sears Plc
Swan Hellenic Ltd
Mr and Ms Daniel Unger
Kurt Unger
Venice Simplon-Orient-Express
Vista Bay Club Seychelles
Vorwerk Carpets Limited
Louis Vuitton Ltd
Warner Bros
White Dove Press
Winsor & Newton
Mrs George Zakhem